POEMS

ON

SEVERAL OCCASIONS.

BY

ELIZABETH RYVES.

LONDON;
PRINTED FOR THE AUTHOR
AND SOLD BY J. DODSLEY, IN PALL

M.DCC.LXXVII.

TO

THE RIGHT HONOURABLE

LORD VISCOUNT BARRINGTON,

SECRETARY AT WAR,

THESE POEMS

ARE RESPECTFULLY INSCRIBED;

BY

His Lordship's

moſt obliged,

moſt obedient,

and moſt humble ſervant,

ELIZABETH RYVES.

SUBSCRIBERS NAMES.

Fnfign Cuff.
Enfign Cunningham.
Mr. Creech, Bookfeller in E-
dinburgh.
Mifs Campbell.
Mr. W. Clement.
Mr. Crips.
Anthony Chamier, Efq;
2 *copies.*
Richard Cox, Efq; 2 *copies.*
Benjamin Cook, Muf. D.
Mr. Jofeph Cripps.
Mrs. Cripps.
Mrs. Carter.
Mifs Carter.
Mrs. Cope.
Mrs. Coates.
John Cowper, Efq;
Frederick Cornewall, Efq;
Mr. Colepoyfe.
Mifs Colepoyfe.
Mr. Caufield.
Mr. Caufield *junior.*
—— Cater, Efq;
Mrs. Cater.
Mifs Cardale.
John Currer, Efq;
Edward Crow, Efq;
Thomas Crow, Efq;
Mrs. Clavering.

D.

Earl of Dumfries. 4 *copies.*
Countefs of Dumfries. 4 *cop.*

Countefs of Dundonald.
John Deffel, Efq;
Mrs. Deffel.
Mifs Deffel.
Mifs Dupree.
Countefs of Denbigh.
Mifs Docwra.
Captain Darby.
Mrs. Darby.
A. Davifon, Efq;
Mr. J. Davifon.
Rev. Robert Dowbiggin,
Sub-Dean of Lincoln.
Henry D'Eftarre, Efq;
Mrs. Doyne.
Rev. Mr. Dodfworth.
Mrs. Dodfworth.
Mrs. Dew.
Charles Warner Dunbar, Efq;
4 *copies.*
Lady Ifabella Douglafs.
Lady Helen Douglafs.
James Dalziel, Efq;
Sir John Duddlefton, Bart.
Enfign Day.
Lieutenant Dogherty.
Lieutenant F. Dogherty.
Lieutenant Dyer.
Captain Drew.
Dr. Duncan.
Mr. Henry Defborough.
Robert Drummond, Efq;
2 *copies.*
Henry Drummond, Efq;
2 *copies.*
William Dinwoody, Efq;
Thomas

SUBSCRIBERS NAMES.

A.

MRS. Armstrong.
    Edward Arthur, Esq;
Miss Arthur.
Mrs. Anstruther.   2 *copies*
Rev. Mr. William Aveling.
Rev. Mr. Thomas Aveling.
William Ayton, Esq;
Mr. William Ayton.
John Ayton, Esq;
George Apthorp, Esq;
John Agnew, Esq;
Nathaniel Agnew, Esq;
Marriot Arbuthnot, Esq;
  4 *copies.*
Mr. William Anderson.
Miss Armstrong.
Mr. Robert Artkin.
Mr. Ashburner.
Thomas Ashe, Esq;
John Ashe, Esq;
Mrs. Ashe.

Miss Ashe.
Miss Anna Maria Achison.
Miss Adderley.
Mr. Atkinson.
Mr. Atwood.
Henry Atherton, Esq;
Mr. James Appleford.

B.

Duchess of Bedford.
Lord Barrington.   4 *copies.*
Francis Brownsmith, Esq;
  2 *copies.*
Mrs. Brownsmith.   2 *copies.*
Mrs. Bird.
Mr. Branson.
Mrs. Blair.
Gregory Bateman, Esq;
Mrs. Brickenden.
Mrs. Beardmore.   2 *copies.*
Brooke Brasier, Esq;

Mrs. Brasier.
Cornet Brasier.
Miss Brasier.
Thomas Butler, Esq; 4 *copies*.
Miss Butler.
Miss Gertude Butler.
J. Barry, Esq;
Mrs. Barry.
Edward Bury, Esq;
Miss Sophia Ann Bury.
Rev. Mr. Burton.
Mr. Burton.
Mrs. Burton.
Lady Bateman. 2 *copies*.
William Brooke, Esq;
Miss Selina Brooke.
Mr. Thomas Bayley.
Mrs. Baugh.
Miss Buck.
Miss Burlton.
Edward Beecher, Esq;
Percival Beaumont, Esq;
Mrs. Beaumont.
Mr. John Beaumont.
Mr. Daniel Beaumont.
Matthew Byndlofs, Esq;
William Baker, Esq;
   20 *copies*.
Mrs. Brandreth.
T. Brandreth, Esq;
Lieutenant Brandreth.
Mrs. Barker. 4 *copies*.
Capt. Thomas Baker.
   2 *copies*.
Mrs. Baker. 2 *copies*.
John Bennet, Esq;

Mrs. Birch.
Mrs. Birch.
Rev. Dr. Barton, Dean of
   Briftol.
Miss Barton.
Capt. Boteler.
Mrs. Bedford.
Rev. Mr. George Beet.
Robert Bunbury, Esq;
   6 *copies*.
Mr. Blank.
Nathaniel Braffey, Esq;
   4 *copies*.
John Bowdler, Esq;
Countefs of Barrymore.
   4 *copies*.
Mrs. Birch. 4 *copies*.
Mr. John Buchan. 2 *copies*.
Rowland Burdon, Esq;
Mr. Walter Boyd.
Mr. George Brown. 2 *copies*.
Dr. Thomas Blacklock.
   6 *copies*.
Mrs. Blair. 4 *copies*.
John Butler, Esq; 4 *copies*.
Richard Bulkley, Esq;
   4 *copies*.
Captain Branfon.
Major Batt.
Enfign Brownrig.
Mr. John Bell. 2 *copies*.
Doctor Blinfhall.
Mr. Braidwood.
Mrs. Baronneau.
Miss Baronneau.
Miss Elizabeth Butts.
                              Mr.

Mr. Baſkerfeild.
Rev. Mr. John Brett.
Miſs Bradbury.
Mrs. Barton.
Colonel Thomas Byren.
Mrs. Bentley.
Tyringham Backwell, Eſq; 2 *copies.*
Mrs. Brohum.
Miſs Brohum.
Mr. James Baverſtock.
W. B. Borwick, Eſq;
George Bevin, Eſq;
Miſs Bevin.

C.

Lady Clive.
Hon. Frederick Cavendiſh. 8 *copies.*
Hon. Mrs. Cochrane.
Mrs. Cotton. 2 *copies.*
Rev. Mr. Clarke.
Mrs. Cooper.
Miſs Cooper.
Mr. Chriſtmas.
Mrs. Cane.
T. Carlton, Eſq;
Mrs. Carlton.
Richard Carey, Eſq;
Mrs. Conner.
Mrs. Coleman.
Nathaniel Clavett, Eſq;
Doctor Cotton.
Rev. Mr. Cotton.
Mr. Claridge.

George Carpenter, Eſq; 2 *copies.*
Michael Cole, Eſq;
Mrs. Cooke.
Mr. Curtis.
Rev. Mr. Cotterel.
William Cowper, Eſq;
Mrs. Curry.
Mrs. Cheſter. 2 *copies.*
Hon. and Rev. Dr. Croſbie, Dean of Limerick.
Rev. Arthur Champagne, Dean of Clonmacnoiſe.
Mrs. Carey.
Mrs. Croker.
Mrs. Cotton.
Maurice O'Conner, Eſq;
Mr. Collings.
Mrs. Conant.
Rt. Hon. Nathaniel Clements, Eſq; 4 *copies.*
S. Clements, Eſq; 2 *copies.*
Mrs. Clements. 2 *copies.*
Mrs. Cookes. 2 *copies.*
Peter Collet, Eſq;
John Collet, Eſq;
Mrs. Copland.
Mr. Hugh Corrie.
Mr. Thomas Cuming. 2 *copies.*
Mr. William Campbell.
Adam Craik, Eſq;
Alexander Copland, Eſq;
Sir George Collier. 4 *copies.*
Lieutenant Collings.
Lieutenant Cary.

Enſign

SUBSCRIBERS NAMES:

Lady Gordon.
Alexander Gordon, Efq;
  2 *copies*.
Gilbert Gordon, Efq;
James Gordon *junior*, Efq;
Mrs. Griffith.
E. Gerey, Efq;
William Gardner, Efq;
George Gardner, Efq;
Mr. Gardner.
Mrs. Gardner.
Mifs Greenfel.
Mrs. Gorges.
Richard Gilpin, Efq;
Rev. Mr. Greaves.
Rev. Mr. Gordon.
Mrs. Gordon,
Arthur Goold, Efq; 4 *copies*.
Mr. Jofeph Goldthwait.
Capt. Griffiths.
Capt. Graves.
Enfign Grant.
Lieut. Gilbert.
Lieut. Graham.
Dr. Gilchrift.
James Guthrie, Efq;
Philip Goodes, Efq; 2 *copies*.
David Garrick, Efq;
Andrew Grote, Efq;
Mr. George Grote.
Rev. Mr. Goodwin.
Mr. Gattingden.
Mrs. Gattingden.
Mrs. Martha Gattingden.
Mr. J. Greenough.
Mr. A. Greenough.
Mrs. Gordon.

Mr. Goodwin.

H.

Hon. Mrs. Hyde.
Dr. Hall.
Mrs. Howe.
Mifs Sarah Holt.
Rev. Mr. Harriot.
Mrs. Rebecca Hide.
Nathaniel Hinde, Efq;
Mrs. Hervey.
Mr. Heatey.
Mifs Hanwell.
William Howard, Efq;
Mifs Hall.
Patrick Heron, Efq; 2 *copies*.
Lady Elizabeth Heron.
  2 *copies*.
Capt. Bafil Heron. 2 *copies*.
Mifs Heron.
Mr. Henry Heron.
Mrs. Hewett. 2 *copies*.
Mifs Hewett.
Mr. Walter Hog.
Thomas Hooper, Efq;
Mifs Henderfon.
Capt. Handfield. 2 *copies*.
Capt. Hanvill.
Capt. Hall.
Mrs. Holland. 4 *copies*.
Lieut. Howe.
Lieut. Hamilton.
Mr. Hatfell.
Mr. Hinchliep.
Mr. James Hatton.
Mr. Hitch.

Mr.

SUBSCRIBERS NAMES.

Thomas Diggle, Efq;
Mifs Sally Denis.
Mrs. Dallow.
Mifs Sally Day.
G. Dalton, Efq;
Mr. Dalton.
Mrs. Dillon.
Rev. Mr. Deacle.
Mifs Sophia Durell.
Mifs Ann Durell.
Mr. Drawfon.
John Dowden, Efq;
Mr. William Dowden.
Mr. Dollman.
Mr. Dring.

E.

Mrs. Eweings.
Mr. Everard.
John Edwards, Efq; 2 *copies.*
Mr. Thomas Everett.
Mrs. Emmet.
Ralph Eaton, Efq;
Mifs S. Evans.
Capt. William Erving.
Mr. George Erving. 2 *copies.*
Lady C. E. 2 *copies.*
Mifs Elliot.
J. Euftace, Efq;
Mr. George Euftace.
Mrs. Caroline Elizabeth Eu-
  ftace.
Capt. Elliot.
Lieut. Elliot.
Lieut. Euftace.
Lieut. Ewing.

Hon. Henry Erfkine.
Mr. Thomas Eldir.
Mr. Elliot, Bookfeller in
  Edinburgh.
Mifs Edgar.
Mr. Eggerton.
Mr. Elmy.

F.

Sir William Forbes, Bart.
  4 *copies.*
Lady Forbes. 4 *copies.*
Capt. Forfter.
Lieut. Fielding. 2 *copies.*
Enfign Forbes.
Mr. Filkes.
Mrs. Filkes.
Rev. Mr. Filkes.
——— Fowler, Efq;
Mrs. Fowler.
Mr. John Fryer.
Mr. Foden.
Mrs. Frederick.
Mr. Fullerton.
Mr. Foot.
Mrs. Freeman.
Mifs Freeman.
Mr. Frafer.
Mifs Fifher.
General Faucitt. 2 *copies.*
William Farquherfon, Efq;
Mrs. Fleming.

G.

Lord Grimfton.
George Goldie, Efq; 4 *copies.*
  Lady

SUBSCRIBERS NAMES.

Miss Awbry Lane.
Mrs. Lovett.
Mr. Langford.
Miss Laurence.
Rev. Dr. Lowe.
Miss Lowe.
Jacob Leroux, Esq;
Mr. John Leroux. 4 *copies*.
Mr. James Lock.
Mr. William Lawson.
John Leslie, Esq;
Capt. Lindsay.
Lieut. Lindsey.
Lieut. Lycett.
Lieut. F. Lewis.
Lieut. J. Lewis.
Mr. Law.
Miss Lowndes.
Miss Mary Lowndes.
Edward Lewis, Esq; 2 *copies*.
Matthew Lewis, Esq; 2 *cop*.
Mr. Lambton.
Mrs. Lambton.
H. Lane, Esq;
Daniel Loring, Esq;
Rich. Ayton Lee, Esq; 2 *cop*.
Mr. Logwood.
Miss Logwood.
Jonathan Lovett, Esq.
Capt. James Leslie.

M.

Countess of Massareen. 2 *cop*.
Lady Rachel Mac Donnel.
  2 *copies*.
Lady Elizabeth Mac Donnel.
  2 *copies*.

Gen. Massey. 4 *copies*.
Mrs. Massey. 4 *copies*.
James Morden, Esq; 4 *copies*.
Capt. Mouatt. 2 *copies*.
Capt. Mackenzie. 2 *copies*.
Capt. Monk.
Capt. Mac Donald.
Capt. Mac Donald, of the
  Marines.
Lieut. Mac Donald.
Lieut. Mathews.
Mr. Jonathan Michie.
Lieut. Moore.
Ensign Morden.
Ensign Mac Donald.
Quarter-Master Mac Donald.
Rev. Mr. Morris.
Miss Millisent.
Mrs. Middleton.
Mrs. Moyser.
Mrs. Murtins.
James Meyrick, Jun. Esq;
Mrs. Mac Neail.
Anthony Malone, Esq;
Mrs. Malone.
Miss Malone.
Mrs. Malone.
Mrs. Malone.
Rev. Mr. Maxwell.
Mrs. Mason.
Capt. Mukins.
Mrs. Mukins.
Capt. Mitchel.
Mrs. Martin.
Mrs. Mackreth.
Mrs. Marshall.
George Muir, Esq; 2 *copies*.
                Lady

SUBSCRIBERS NAMES,

Mr. Thomas Heathfield,
Lieut. Haviland.
Mr. Hill.
Mr. Howe.
Mrs. Hamilton.
James Hunter, Esq;
Rev. Mr. Hawkins.
Mr. John Hollingworth.
Mrs. Hollingworth.
Mr. Hallowell.
Rev. Mr. Holberry.
Miss Bridget Hoare. ◯
Miss Hallifax.
Mr. Hill.
T. Higgins, Esq;
Mr. Richard Howe.
Sir John Hales, Bart. 2 *cop.*
Samuel Haywood, Esq;
John Haywood, Esq; 2 *cop.*
Mrs. Harris.
Thomas Harris, Esq;
Miss Hall.

I.

Rev. Mr. Jephcott.
Rev. Mr. Jephcott, *junior.*
Mrs. Elizabeth Jackson.
John Irving, Esq;
Mr. Richard Jago.
Miss Isherwood.
Miss Johnson.
Miss Ireson.
William Jackson, Esq; 2 *cop.*
Patrick Johnson, Esq;
William Johnson, Esq;
Dr. Jefferys.

Capt. Johnson.
Capt. J. Johnson.
Lieut. Jacobs.
Rev. Mr. Jenkins.   2 *copies.*
James Pygott Ince, Esq;
Mrs. Jowett.

K.

Capt. Kingsmill.
William Ker, Esq;   4 *copies,*
Mrs. Kirby.
Thomas Knight, Esq;
Mr. Thomas King.
Mr. William King.
Rev. Mr. Keller.
Benjamin Kidney, Esq;
Mrs. Kidney.
Miss Sarah Knowler.
Miss Knightley.

L.

Mr. Herbert Laurence.
Rev. Mr. Lettice.   4 *copies.*
Lady Leith.   2 *copies.*
Miss Lambport.
Mrs. Lewis.
Edward Lake, Esq;
Mrs. Laffells.
D. Lawson, Esq;
Miss Long.
Miss Lloyd.
Edward Llewellin, Esq;
Mrs. Llewellin.
Mrs. Lloyd.
Mrs. Lewinworth.
John Lloyd, Esq;

Miss

SUBSCRIBERS NAMES.

Miss Awbry Lane.
Mrs. Lovett.
Mr. Langford.
Miss Laurence.
Rev. Dr. Lowe.
Miss Lowe.
Jacob Leroux, Esq;
Mr. John Leroux. 4 copies.
Mr. James Lock.
Mr. William Lawson.
John Leslie, Esq;
Capt. Lindsay.
Lieut. Lindsey.
Lieut. Lycett.
Lieut. F. Lewis.
Lieut. J. Lewis.
Mr. Law.
Miss Lowndes.
Miss Mary Lowndes.
Edward Lewis, Esq; 2 copies.
Matthew Lewis, Esq; 2 cop.
Mr. Lambton.
Mrs. Lambton.
H. Lane, Esq;
Daniel Loring, Esq;
Rich. Ayton Lee, Esq; 2 cop.
Mr. Logwood.
Miss Logwood.
Jonathan Lovett, Esq.
Capt. James Leslie.

M.

Countess of Massareen. 2 cop.
Lady Rachel Mac Donnel.
  2 copies.
Lady Elizabeth Mac Donnel.
  2 copies.

Gen. Massey. 4 copies.
Mrs. Massey. 4 copies.
James Morden, Esq; 4 copies.
Capt. Mouatt. 2 copies.
Capt. Mackenzie. 2 copies.
Capt. Monk.
Capt. Mac Donald.
Capt. Mac Donald, of the
  Marines.
Lieut. Mac Donald.
Lieut. Mathews.
Mr. Jonathan Michie.
Lieut. Moore.
Ensign Morden.
Ensign Mac Donald.
Quarter-Master Mac Donald.
Rev. Mr. Morris.
Miss Millisent.
Mrs. Middleton.
Mrs. Moyser.
Mrs. Murtins.
James Meyrick, Jun. Esq;
Mrs. Mac Neail.
Anthony Malone, Esq;
Mrs. Malone.
Miss Malone.
Mrs. Malone.
Mrs. Malone.
Rev. Mr. Maxwell.
Mrs. Mason.
Capt. Mukins.
Mrs. Mukins.
Capt. Mitchel.
Mrs. Martin.
Mrs. Mackreth.
Mrs. Marshall.
George Muir, Esq; 2 copies.
                              Lady

SUBSCRIBERS NAMES.

Lady Maxwell. 2 *copies.*
James Mounſey, Eſq; 2 *cop.*
Mrs. Mounſey.
Miſs Mounſey.
James Mackey, Eſq;
Mrs. Moriſon.
Robert Maxwell, Eſq;
Mr. Neil Marvier.
Mr. Mackey.
Mrs. Munn.
Capt. Mackenzie.
William Mills, Eſq;
Mrs. Margetſon.
David Martin, Eſq;

N.

Mrs. Noel.
F. Newman, Eſq;
Mr. Newton.
Mrs. Nicol.
Mrs. Naſh.
Mrs. Nugent.
John Newall, Eſq;
Archibald Nidjen, Eſq;
Mr. Nuttleworth.
Mrs. Nuttleworth.
Miſs Neſbitt.
Miſs Lucy Neſbitt.
Mr. Robert Nixon.
Mr. John Nixon.
Mrs. Nettles.

O.

Earl of Oſſory. 2 *copies.*

Counteſs of Oſſory. 2 *copies.*
Henry Obrien, Eſq;
Mrs. Obrien.
Mr. Obrien.
Miſs Obrien.
Mrs. Oſborne. 4 *copies.*
Robert Oliphant, Eſq; 2 *cop.*
W. Oliver, Eſq;
Mr. Oliver.
Mrs. Oſborne.
Mrs. Oſborne.
Mrs. Orbey.
Mr. Ormſby.
Miſs Ormſby.
Mr. Otter.
Mr. Edward Otter,

P.

Lady Caroline Peachy.
Mrs. Paſham.
Mrs. Pytts.
Capt. Pool.
Mrs. Pittman.
Rev. Mr. Preedy.
Miſs Preedy.
Miſs Powles.
Mrs. Pearce.
Mrs. Paulham.
Mrs. Purrier.
Rev. Mr. Pearkes.
Rev. Mr. Proſſer.
William Pembroke, Eſq;
Miſs Pemberton.
Mrs. Pomfret.

Miſs

Miss Pell.

Christopher Potter, Esq;

Miss Petty.

General Pigot.

Col. Pringle.

Capt. Perceval.

Capt. Pitcairn.

James Portens, Esq; *4 copies.*

Mr. Philips. *2 copies.*

Mr. John Perkins.

Sir William Pepperell, Bart.
  4 copies.

Miss Constantia Pargeter.

Mrs. Prowse. *4 copies.*

Rev. Mr. Pitts.

Mr. Pritchard.

Mrs. Pauncefort.

Mr. Palmer.

Mr. Prevett.

Miss Pinkney.

Miss Price.

Thomas Powell, Esq; *4 cop.*

Rev. Mr. Purefoy.

Mrs. Paulin.

Edward Parker, Esq;

Thomas Parker, Esq;

H. Parker, Esq;

Mrs. Parker.

Mr. Parker.

Miss Parker.

Mrs. Parkes.

Mrs. Jane Parkes.

Mr. Pulham.

Miss Pulham.

Miss Juliana Pulham.

Mrs. Potter.

Mrs. Prescott.

Miss Prescott.

Mrs. Purvis.

Miss Purvis.

Miss Pierce.

Mr. Paulhan.

Q.

J. Quin, Esq;

Mr. Quin.

Mrs. Quin.

Mr. Thomas Quirk.

Mrs. Mary Quirk.

R.

Right Hon. Richard Rigby,
  Esq; *2 copies.*

Mrs. Rundell. *2 copies.*

Colonel Rawson.

Capt. Ramsey.

Capt. Ross.

Capt. Rooke.

Mr. Reynolds.

Rev. Mr. Richards.

John Routhedge, Esq;

Thomas Reeve, Esq;

Miss Ross.

Miss Roebuck.

Mr. Charles Robertson.

Mr. John Rutherford.

Miss Ramsey.

Mrs. Ann Reynardson.

Mr. Rowley.

Mr. Thomas Rowley.

Mrs. Richardson.

Miss Richardson.

Mr.

SUBSCRIBERS NAMES.

Mr. Robinson.
Mr. Robinson *junior*.
Mrs. Ridgway.
William Rowe, Esq;
Mr. Rowe.
Mr. Henry Rowe.
Miss Rowe.
Miss Rose.
Miss Catherine Rose.
Charles Justinian Rainsford,
  Esq;
Mrs. Russel.
Mr. Rouse.
Mrs. Robinson,

S.

Countess Spencer.
Countess of Selkirk.
Mr. Spencer.
Mr. Stolt.
Major Studholm. 4 *copies*.
Major Souter. 4 *copies*.
Capt. Spry. 4 *copies*.
Lieut. Sims.
Lieut. Stewart.
Capt. Stirling.
Capt. Smith.
Lieut. Soloman.
Lieut. Short.
Lieut. Shea.
Ensign St. George. 8 *copies*.
Quarter-Master Smith.
Mr. Servant.
Mr. Silver.
Lady Catherine Skeffington.

—— Sneyd, Esq; 2 *copies*.
Miss Lucy Savage.
Thomas Sheppard, Esq;
Mrs. Sheppard.
Mrs. Sheppard *senior*.
Miss Shipton.
Sir William St. Quintin, Bart.
John Selvey, Esq;
Mr. Robert Smith.
Miss Salter.
Mrs. Smith.
Mrs. Elizabeth Searancke.
Rev. Mr. Scott.
Edward Smith, Esq;
Mrs. Smith.
Rev. Mr. Symonds.
Dr. Stubbe.
Rev. Mr. James Smyth.
John Sterling, Esq;
Miss Sterling.
Dr. Daniel Smith.
Mrs. Caroline Ann Sabine.
Mrs. St. George.
Dr. Shearer.
George Stepney, Esq;
Mrs. Stepney.
Philip Rawson Stepney,
  Esq;
Mr. Sargent.
Mr. H. Styleman.
Mr. Strut.
Mr. John Sandon.
Mrs. Saffory.
Miss Strut.
Mr. S. H. Sparhawk.
Mrs. Scott.
Mr. John Syme. 2 *copies*.

Hon.

Hon. Kieth Stewart.
Mr. William Scott.
Lady Stewart.
James Sterling, Efq;
Mr. Andrew Stewart.
Mifs Scott.
Mr. Samborn.
John Searancke, Efq;
Mrs. Searancke.
William Southwell, Efq;
  2 copies.
Mrs. Southwell.   2 copies.
Mifs Sparrow.
Mifs Scriven.
Mifs Stracy.
Mrs. Skevington.
Mrs. Stephens.
Mifs Stephens.
Mr. Stoney.
Mr. Arthur Stoney.
Mr. Staines.   2 copies.
Mr. Smyth.
Col. Skey.
Mr. Sevigny.
Henry Scott, Efq;

Mifs Tapps.
John Bigge Thornton, Efq;
Chriftopher Tower, Efq;
Mrs. Tower.
Mifs Ann Taylor.
Thomas Thompfon, Efq;
Mrs. Turner.
Mrs. Elizabeth Terry. 6 cop,
Mr. John Towfe.
Lieut. Trollope.
Rev. Mr. Tiley.
Mrs. Traverfe.
Mifs Traverfe.

U.

Mrs. Uthwatt.
Mrs. Underwood.
Rev. Mr. Vickers.
Thomas Vaux, Efq; 4 copies,
Jofeph Vandermulen, Efq;
Mr. Vernon.
Mrs. Vernon.
James Villers, Efq;
Mifs Villers.

T.

Rev. Mr. Tanquery. 2 copies.
—— Turner, Efq;
Mrs. Turner.
Mr. Travanion.
Mr. W. Thorne.
John Thorp, Efq;
Mr. John Thomas.
Mrs. Throckmorton.
Mrs. Thompfon.

W.

Richard Williams, Efq;
Mrs. Wade.
Mifs Wade.
Mifs Windham.
Mr. John Whitehead.
Mr. Wanfey.
Mr. Wallace.
Mr. Wells,

Mifs

SUBSCRIBERS NAMES.

Mifs Waller.
Mifs Grace Waller.
Mrs. Wilkins.
Mifs Wilkins.
Mrs. Wetherell.
The Ladies of Mrs. Wetherell's School.
Mifs Winter.
Mr. Charles Wetherell.
Rev. Mr. Wheeldon. 4 *copies*.
Mr. Winkfield.
Rev. Mr. Watkin.
James Warren, Efq;
Mifs Warren.
Mifs H. G. White.
Mifs Whifton.
Mr. Warren.
Mr. Whitbread.
Mr. Andrew Wood. 2 *copies*.
Mrs. Wright. 6 *copies*.
Rev. Mr. Willis. 2 *copies*.
Wadham Wyndham, Efq;
Helyar Wadham Wyndham, Efq;
Capt. Wade. 4 *copies*.
Capt. Weft.
Lieut. Waller.

Lieut. Welfh.
Mr. Woolfe.
Mr. Alexander Wood.
Mrs. Winbolt.
Mrs. Williamfon.
Mifs Williamfon.
Mifs Whitfield.
Mifs Wright.
John Williams, Efq;
Mr. Williams.
Capt. Waring.
Mrs. White.
Mifs White.
Mr. Whittworth.
James Whiting, Efq;
Mifs Sophia Whiting.
Capt. Ward.
Mr. Winkley.
Mifs Wellwood.

Y.

Mrs. Young.
Mr. Yelverton.
Mr. George Yelverton.

C O N T E N T S.

CONTENTS.

POEMS.

P O E M S.

THE TWO FOLLOWING POEMS
WERE PRESENTED TO THE KING,
WITH A PETITION,
IN MAY 1775.

HAIL gracious Monarch! whose extensive sway
    Climes far remote and distant realms obey;
Where the rude natives, savage as their soil,
Nurtur'd in danger and enur'd to toil,
Already form'd by thy paternal care,
And lur'd from all the rough pursuits of war,
Revere the sceptre in thy ruling hand,
And yield obedient to thy mild command.
To thee, with virtue as with glory crown'd,
For mercy honour'd as in arms renown'd;
To thee Affliction for relief applies;
Oh hear with pity, nor her suit despise!

B   Sprung

Sprung from a Sire, whose generous soul disdain'd
The softer scenes where Peace and Pleasure reign'd;
Where smiling Ease led on the tranquil hours,
'Midst his paternal plains and native bow'rs;
Where Reason strove to calm each wild desire,
Confine the views of youth and moderate its fire:
But vain the task—his bosom burn'd for fame,
The laurel crown, the hero's honour'd name.
Nor rural shades, or youthful sports could please;
Inglorious those appear'd, ignoble these;
And, ere cool Judgment lent her steady ray,
Ambition taught his heedless steps to stray.

Full thirty years he join'd the martial train,
And dar'd each danger of the hostile plain;
Till worn with toils, ere nature fix'd his doom,
The soldier sunk into the silent tomb.
" The day that to the shades the father sends,
" Robs the sad orphan of her father's friends.
" She, wretched outcast of mankind, appears
" For ever sad, for ever drown'd in tears.
" Among the happy, unregarded she
" Hangs on the robe, or trembles at the knee;
" While those her father's former bounty fed,
" Nor reach the goblet or divide the bread."
                                            Thus

Thus Homer fung the ills which I deplore;
No friend to lend affiftance, or reftore
The orphan's birthright, or the widow's dow'r.
While proud Oppreffion triumphs in their cares,
Laughs at their forrows, and infults their tears;
And, arm'd with wealth, (the villain's boafted pow'r)
Wrefts from their hands the birthright and the
    dow'r.

May'ft thou, dread Sov'reign, to my pray'r attend,
While humbly proftrate at thy throne I bend!
Oh may my tears thy royal bofom move
My wrongs to pity, and my fuit approve!
While I, ambitious of immortal fame,
Adorn my fong with thy illuftrious name.
Since mufic, painting, ev'ry lib'ral art
Which forms the manners or improves the heart,
Thy royal bounty fhares, and boldly tries
From ancient Greece to wreft the doubtful prize;
Since ev'ry Mufe, invited by thy fmile,
Leaves Tiber's banks for thy more favour'd ifle,
And bids Britannia boaft immortal fame,
Great as th' Athenian or the Roman name;
May I, the meaneft of the tuneful choir,
To fhare thy bounty and thy fmiles afpire!

No

No title I pretend, no specious plea;
Compassion only claims the boon for me.
To her, relenting, my rude verse excuse,
And hear the suppliant, tho' thou scorn the Muse.
So may just Heav'n on thee its blessings show'r, ⎤
Extend thy conquests, and support thy pow'r, ⎬
And crown with circling joys each future hour. ⎦'
May guardian angels from thy foes defend; ⎤
May peace and plenty on thy reign attend; ⎬
And as thy virtues, may thy bliss transcend! ⎦

O D E.

O D E.

SILENT my voice, my lute unftrung
  Neglected on a drooping cyprefs hung;
Or tun'd (while penfive Melancholy reign'd)
In concert with the heaving figh,
The agonizing heart, the ftreaming eye,
Of hard oppreffion and of wrongs complain'd;
Till the prophetic God infpir'd,
And bade Imagination tow'r
Beyond where fortune frowns or tempefts lowr.
Where fate unfolds the fcene from fenfe conceal'd,
And dark futurity's at once reveal'd.

Thus, by the Mufe inflam'd, I fweep the lyre,
While Britain's future glories meet my eyes;
Bid the pale train of gloomy cares retire,
And leave me free to range the diftant fkies.
My wrongs recede, I hail the favour'd ifle,
And in the midft of wayward fortunes fmile.

Hark! in Fancy's magic ear
The voice of Albion's guardian God I hear,

B 3   Loud

Loud as the found of the tempeftuous main,
When Neptune, rous'd to war,
O'er foaming Ocean drives his thund'ring car,
And fhakes the folid Earth thro' its extended reign.

" Hence, jarring Difcord, to the realms below;
" Hence, and avoid the meditated blow.
" Offspring of Hell, no more prefume
" To rife beyond the Stygian gloom;
" But deep in chaos and eternal night,
" Seek the dark covert of confufion's womb;
" And there in black oblivion hide
" Thy train of mifchiefs, till the gen'ral doom.

Thus fpoke the Genius who prefides
O'er Albion's fhores and her furrounding tides.
Fierce Nemefis attends the angry God,
And brandifhes her fnaky rod
O'er the infernal brood.
Aw'd by the ftern beheft and threat'ning hand,
Faction drops her fiery brand;
And bold Sedition, trembling at the found,
Feels the dread avenging wound,
As down fhe finks to the Tartarian flood.

7

Again

Again the guardian Pow'r refumes
The facred mandate from on high;
Pois'd proudly on ambrofial plumes,
While awful thunders rend the fky,
Refponfive to the Deity.
" Britannia, emprefs of the waves, arife;
" The charm's diffolv'd, the fpell is broke,
" Which bound thy fons to Faction's tyrant yoke.
" Britons are free, Fate ratifies the doom
" To nations yet unborn, and ages ftill to come."
The rocks, the woods, reverberate the found;
In murmurs ev'ry flowing ftream replies;
From pole to pole fhrill Echo fhouts around,
" Britannia, emprefs of the waves, arife !"

Deep in the bofom of the main,
Where hoary Neptune holds his ancient court,
Britannia and her fifter-train
Of fea-born Nereids fport.
Some roll the waves in wanton play;
Some on the backs of dolphins ride;
Some the wild rage of rifing ftorms allay,
And fome controul the tide:
Till thro' the deep receffes of the flood,
Th' immortal voice refounding,
From cave to cave rebounding

Like

Like echo'd thunder, fills the deep abode.
Fir'd with the found, Britannia leaves
The coral bow'rs, the pearly caves,
And on the Albion ftrand
Réfumes her throne and fceptre of command.
Trophies of war fpontaneous rife,
Rich with the fpoils of many a glorious prize;
While her fam'd ftandard borne on high,
Secure of future victory,
Floats proudly on the air, and brightens all the fky.

" Genius of Albion, guardian of my ifle,
" Bright delegate of the immortal Pow'rs;
" Whofe frown can awe, and whofe benignant
    " fmile
" Calms the wild tumult that around me lowrs:
" Refcu'd by thee, Britons no more fhall feel
" The vain delufions Jealoufy infpires;
" But mutual faith fecure their mutual weal,
" And blended int'refts banifh Faction's fires:
" While their dread Monarch, with paternal hand,
" Nor rules fevere, nor flackens in command;
" But guides his fteady courfe with juft applaufe,
" And guards their rights, their honour, and their
    " laws."

The

The Goddefs thus addrefs'd the guardian Pow'r,
While Jove, low bending from his bright abode,
Bade the aufpicious thunders roar,
And ftamp'd the mandate with an awful nod.
The deities who round his throne attend,
Swift heralds of th' eternal will, obey;
And wing'd with rapid fpeed defcend
(Urging their courfe thro' heav'n's refplendent way)
Where the dire Sifters ply their fatal loom,
And in its various tiffue weave the great events to
    come.

Intent on Britain's future fame,
Her rifing glory, her immortal name,
With ready hands, th' obedient Fates prepare
Soft fhades of peace to blend with fcenes of war;
And as the bufy fhuttle flies,
Fair views of commerce fpread, and diftant conquefts
    rife.

Soon on the azure field embofs'd is feen,
With flags difplay'd and fails unfurl'd,
Riding in triumph, Britain's bold marine,
Prepar'd to hail her Emprefs of the World.
And there in bright array her legions ftand,
Gallant as thofe in Poicters' glorious field,

                    Which

Which bade proud Gaul's infulting tyrant yield,
And own his conquer'd crown the boon of Edward's
    hand.
Firm like the rocks which bound their native
    fhore,
And frown defiance to the waves and wind,
They ftand unmov'd amidft furrounding war,
And mock the force of leaguing realms combin'd.

But whither tow'rs my daring Mufe?
Let Man, by nature form'd to wield
The glitt'ring falchion, and to grafp the fhield,
Skill'd in the rougher arts of war,
A pencil dipt in ftronger tints prepare;
While I, retiring, chufe a fofter fhade,
Where Peace, and Wealth, and Plenty, ftand dif-
    play'd;
Where the deep-loaded barks are feen,
Fraught with the treafure of each diftant fhore;
At anchor there they ride, there fkim the main,
Enrich'd with Afric's gold, and India's fpicy ftore.

Thefe, Britain, be thy glory, thefe thy pride;
Let Commerce fpread the fwelling fails;
Fortune will grant aufpicious gales,
And riches flow on each returning tide.
                  Such

Such are the bleffings which await
Obedient fubjects and a tranquil ftate;
And fuch the favours Heav'n prepares
To crown a monarch's hopes, a nation's ardent
    pray'rs.

ODE

O D E
T O
S E N S I B I L I T Y.

I.

THE ſordid wretch who ne'er has known,
   To feel for miſeries not his own;
Whoſe lazy pulſe ſerenely beats,
While injur'd worth her wrongs repeats;
Dead to each ſenſe of joy or pain,
A uſeleſs link in nature's chain,
May boaſt the calm which I diſdain.

II.

Give me a generous ſoul, that glows
With others' tranſports, others' woes;
Whoſe noble nature ſcorns to bend,
Tho' Fate her iron ſcourge extend:
But bravely bears the galling yoke,
And ſmiles ſuperior to the ſtroke,
With ſpirit free and mind unbroke.

Yet,

III.

Yet, by compaſſion touch'd, not fear,
Sheds the ſoft ſympathizing tear,
In tribute to Affliction's claim,
Or envy'd Merit's wounded fame.
Let Stoics ſcoff! I'd rather be
Thus curſt with Senſibility,
Than ſhare their boaſted Apathy.

THE
PROGRESS
OF
ENVY.

A FRAGMENT.

IN days of yore, as fages fing,
   When nature own'd immortal fpring;
When flow'ry meads and woodlands green,
Thro' circling feafons grac'd the fcene;
Ere fhadowy clouds or wint'ry gloom
Had ftole upon the vernal bloom,
Or blighting tempefts learn'd to blow,
Or Eurus fledg'd his wings with fnow;
Content maintain'd her gentle reign,
Sweet guardian of the wide domain.
To her the rural chieftains bow'd;
The Mufes fung, the lovers vow'd;
And at the Goddefs' honour'd fhrine
Each nymph her freedom did refign:

While

While Jealoufy, and all her train
Of pale fufpicions, fled the fane;
For when content the heart infpires,
And guards it from delufive fires,
No anxious cares gay Hymen knows;
No anguifh wounds his foft repofe.

Stern Difcord, with her dire alarms
Of hiffing arrows, clanging arms;
Her rattling fhield, her thundering car,
And all the horrid din of war,
In this blefs'd region then unknown,
Ne'er pamper'd pride, or fhook the throne.

Their morals found, their manners chafte,
Their pleafures pure, and juft their tafte;
No languid taper's fickly blaze
Supply'd the fun's departed rays;
No frantic revel, midnight dance,
Which bid untimely age advance,
(Sources of forrow and difeafe)
As yet had learn'd the art to pleafe.
No friendlefs orphan mourn'd her fire,
Deluded by ambition's fire;
No widow'd matron wept her lord,
Sad victim of a hoftile fword;
No giddy youth impoverifh'd lay,
The gamefter's or the wanton's prey;

No

No gentle nymph, condemn'd to mourn,
Invok'd her vagrant love's return :
But smiling peace, and blooming health,
And innocence, their choicest wealth;
With sprightly mirth, in smiles array'd,
On ev'ry face were seen pourtray'd.

From murky regions veil'd in clouds,
Where Vice her hideous aspect shrouds,
With looks askaunt, and haggard eyen,
Pale Envy view'd the tranquil scene;
And, sick'ning at the soft repose
Which from content and virtue flows,
Tho' half impeded by despair,
To Jove addrefs'd her guilty pray'r :
" Oh thou, whose partial will decrees
" The flow'ry spring, the fragrant breeze,
" And all the vary'd joys that wait
" To bless yon new creation's state ;
" Why, favouring thus the upstart race,
" Does Jove diffuse celestial grace ?
" Why wing each gale with sweet perfume ?
" Why paint their vales with Eden's bloom?
" Why give them all the heart requires,
" Ambition seeks, or hope desires ?

" The

" The smiling Graces there resort;
" There Phœbus, there the Muses sport,
" And sweetly swell the choral lay,
" As Pan or Ceres claim the day;
" While woods and waves their notes prolong,
" And list'ning Gods applaud the song.
  " But (exil'd) I'm compell'd to stray,
" As threat'ning tempests urge my way,
" To scenes where wild Confusion reigns,
" Where Night and Chaos dash their chains;
" Where Malice whets her secret steel,
" And smiles Detraction's stings conceal;
" Where smooth Hypocrisy is seen
" With ranc'rous heart, tho' specious mien;
" Where fierce Revenge his poniard steeps
" In kindred gore, while nature sleeps;
" Where Jealousy, whose baleful eye
" Can guilt in innocence descry,
" Broods o'er imaginary cares,
" And tortures for herself prepares;
" Where Anger grinds his iron jaws,
" And fell Remorse her entrails gnaws,
" Urg'd by her co-mate, wild Despair,
" Whom Fear forbids th' attoning pray'r.
  " Thus mark'd by Jove's relentless ire,
" In vain I plead, in vain aspire,

.C   " To

" To thefe infernal depths I'm doom'd,
" With Hell's mad progeny inhum'd;
" And, fir'd with rage and baffled pride,
" Still curfe the bleffings I'm deny'd.
 " If dread Saturnius guides his fway,
" As Juftice marks the equal way,
" Let me no more of wrongs complain,
"' Or partial Providence arraign;
" But in the new creation fhare,
" And breathe the fweets of temp'rate air."

Aftonifh'd Gods th' event attend,
While fighs convulfive Nature rend;
Till Jove low bending from on high,
With floods of glory fill'd the fky.
Sublime in wrath the God look'd down,
While thunders hail'd his awful frown;
And with a ftern, a threat'ning glance,
Check'd the afpiring Fiend's advance,
And angry fpoke:
 " Daughter of Hell, thy daring pray'r,
" Abafh'd at Jove's command, forbear;
" And deep in Stygian darknefs fhroud
" Thy guilt from an offended God."

Not

Not fo repuls'd, fhe thus replies,
(While lowring clouds involve the fkies,
Dark omens of approaching woes
The fatal record foon difclofe)
" Since vengeful Jove difdains my caufe,
" I fpurn his pow'r, reject his laws;
" On the behefts of Fate prefume,
" And thence demand a milder doom."

The Thunderer heard the dread appeal,
And bade the Fates their book reveal ;
Where fuch appears the firm decree,
From which not Gods themfelves are free,
That Envy, wide as air, may prey,
And rav'ning wing her baleful way.
    The immortal volumes thus difplay'd,
Jove their relentlefs doom obey'd,
And with a voice which fhook the fkies,
Reluctant, bade the Fiend arife.
    The Fiend arofe—with haggard mien
And threat'ning fhriek fhe hail'd the fcene ;
While each infernal demon round,
In hideous yells return'd the found.
    Now favage joy in chaos reigns,
The hifs of fnakes, the clank of chains ;

Stormy

Stormy winds that burſt their caves,
Rattling hail, and roaring waves;
Broken thunders taught to jar,
Shocks of elemental war,
At once in mad confuſion riſe,
And with harſh diſcord grate the ſkies.
Anger to revel ſoon ſucceeds;
Each on the other's poniard bleeds:
While Envy, from the frantic crew
By her inflam'd, exulting flew;
Thro' floods and fires ſhe bent her flight,
And left the realms of endleſs night;
Brooding deſtruction in her way,
She reach'd the orient bounds of day:
And, leſt that hideous form ſhould ſcare
The prey from her infernal ſnare,
A martial mien the Fiend aſſumes,
And ſhades her withering brow with plumes:
Rich purple garments half enfold
Her cuiraſs bright with burniſh'd gold;
And, form'd to flow with graceful pride,
Adorn the mail they ſeem to hide.
A maſſy ſhield of ample ſize,
Brac'd on her arm, each dart defies;
And radiant ſword of temper try'd,
Enrich'd with gems, adorns her ſide:

Her

Her cheek, where warlike ardour glows,
Her gorgeous robe, which loofely flows,
Her quivering fpear, her lofty creft,
Proclaim Ambition's form confefs'd.
Proud of the new, the gay difguife,
With daring flight fhe tempts the fkies;
Triumphant waves her wide-fpread wings,
And thro' the realms of æther fprings.

THREE

THREE ELEGIES,

WRITTEN IN DECEMBER, 1776.

ELEGY THE FIRST,

LAVINIA to GALLUS,

I.

LET fordid nymphs, by vain ambition led,
    Purfue thofe paths where pride directs the way;
For titled fools the lure of beauty fpread,
And court falfe fplendor impotently gay.

II.

In fome lone fhade, fome calm fequefter'd grove,
Where Friendfhip rears her unpolluted fhrine,
Sacred to chafte delights and mutual love,
To dwell with thee in fweet content be mine.

III. There,

III.

There, when the rofy morn falutes our bow'r,
And bleating flocks invite us to arife,
Shouldft thou indulge in fleep the breezy hour,
And flumbers loiter on thy drowfy eyes;

IV.

With willing care preventing thy defire,
Swift to the fold with bufy hafte I'll fly,
And ere pale twilight's ling'ring fhades retire,
A fhepherd's duty to thy flocks fupply:

V.

Releafe them from their nightly pen, or bear
The new-fall'n lamb upon my bofom home;
Then to thy couch with anxious fpeed repair,
Left thou fhouldft wake, and chide my early roam.

VI.

But flumbering ftill, I'll hang enamour'd o'er
Thy manly graces, fteal a tender kifs;
Gazing like mifers on their treafur'd ftore,
Source of their hopes, and fpring of all their blifs.

VII.

Or, if uneafy dreams thy fleep prolong,
And haunt thee with imaginary woes,
I'll chafe the hovering fhadows with my fong,
And lull thee on my bofom to repofe.

C 4 VIII. Or,

VIII.

Or, fondly leaning on thy arm, repair
To prune the wild luxuriance of our bow'r ;
Where new-blown woodbines fcent the balmy air,
And fweeter jeff'mines fpread their infant flow'r.

IX.

There, as the waving branches we entwine,
'Tis thine to blend inftruction with our toil ;
To teach how plants with richer foliage fhine,
By art adapted to each varying foil.

X.

Shew why the violet loves a moffy bank,
Why fairer lilies chufe a fhelt'ring fhade,
Why iris blooms midft fedge and oziers dank,
While primrofe-bloffoms paint the upland glade,

XI.

Thence gently rifing to a nobler fphere,
The heav'nly fyftem in my view you bring ;
Defcribe each circling planet's wide career,
And bid me foar on contemplation's wing.

XII.

While I, enraptur'd with the glorious fcene,
Thy manly eloquence fublimely draws,
In fancy range along the radiant fheen,
And think each lift'ning angel fmiles applaufe.

XIII. Oft

XIII.

Oft too, at evening's calm return, we'll ftray
Where arching poplars yon fmooth rill embow'r,
While filver moon-beams on the current play,
And dewy zephyrs hail the tranquil hour.

XIV.

(There penfive thought and foft reflection reign;
No unharmonious found difturbs the fhade;
No tumult dares the peaceful fcene profane;
No favage feet the verdant path invade.

XV.

Secure, the plumy fongfters of the grove
There early build and nurfe the callow brood,
And, grateful for the fhelt'ring fhade, improve
With chearful notes the murmurs of the flood.)

XVI.

Till filent birds, and Cynthia's fwift decline,
To the known cottage urge our homeward way,
Where Hymen's torches with full luftre fhine,
And peace and innocence attend his fway.

ELEGY

ELEGY THE SECOND.

The COMPLAINT.

I.

SILENCE ye rills, ye zephyrs ceafe to blow;
Thou love-lorn Philomel fufpend thy fong;
Soft echo only fhall repeat my woe,
And, fighing, waft the mournful tale along.

II.

Gallus no more revifits thofe fweet fhades,
No more returns to blefs my widow'd arms;
My lute grows ufelefs, and my beauty fades,
While Gallus gazes on fome rival's charms.

III.

Where are thofe looks of unfufpected love,
Thofe fpecious fmiles, and that enchanting voice,
When Gallus call'd each lift'ning Pow'r above,
To hear his vows and ratify his choice?

IV. Difpers'd

IV.

Difpers'd like morning-dew, no trace remains,
Save in Lavinia's poor neglected heart ;
While fhe, fond mourner, wears her tyrant's chains,
Broods o'er her woes, and cherifhes the fmart.

V.

Thou Sacred Pow'r, beneath whofe awful dome
Our faith was plighted, and our hands were join'd ;
Perfuafive Love, recall my wanderer home,
And fix thofe bands thou didft fo fweetly bind !

VI.

Paint his Lavinia's eyes diffolv'd in tears,
Imploring Heav'n to fpare her vagrant fpoufe ;
For him fhe pleads, for him, alas ! fhe fears,
Left angry Fate avenge his faithlefs vows.

VII.

Defcribe that foft folicitude which flows
From tendernefs and grief, when both tranfcend ;
No fierce refentment my fond bofom knows ;
I mourn my hufband, and bewail my friend.

VIII.

Anger with love fure never yet agreed,
Or in one heart maintain'd a jarring fhrine :
Softnefs prevails where juftice dares not plead ;
Then ftill to weep and fupplicate be mine.

ELEGY

ELEGY THE THIRD.

The COMPLAINT, continued.

To GALLUS.

I.

ME not the balmy breath of morn can pleafe,
    Tho' rofy Phœbus wakes the flow'ry plain;
Or noon-tide fhade, or evening's fragrant breeze,
Or dewy-pinion'd twilight's fhadowy reign.

II.

For me in vain the fportive younglings play;
In vain for me the birds foft warbles trill:
Languid and pale, with heedlefs fteps I ftray
Along the lawn, or up the pine-crown'd hill;

III.

My penfive eyes revolving fondly o'er
Thofe haunts where peace and Gallus lately ftray'd;
Where he, deep-vers'd in wifdom's facred lore,
Her polifh'd truths in love's foft founds convey'd.

IV. Learning

IV.

Learning and sense, without pedantic art,
So easy flow'd from his accomplish'd tongue;
Each precept stole on my attentive heart,
Sweet and instructive as Urania's song.

V.

The dear impression still my soul deceives;
In fancy yet his charming voice I hear,
If but a passing zephyr fans the leaves,
Or distant rill's mild murmur strikes my ear.

VI.

Thence wing'd imagination takes its flight;
I share the tender kiss by him imprefs'd,
Hang on his accents still with sweet delight,
And in idea am supremely blest:

VII.

Thus, Gallus, I my anxious hours deceive,
Thus fondly paint the visionary scene:
Awhile the flattering shadows I believe;
My sighs are silenc'd, and my heart's serene.

VIII.

But soon those gay delusions lose their charms;
Soon reason penetrates the kind deceit;
My fears describe thee in a rival's arms,
And ev'ry languid pulse forgets to beat.

THE

THE

TRIUMPH of HYMEN:

A MASK.

ADDRESSED TO A NOBLEMAN,

ON HIS MARRIAGE.

ACT the FIRST.

The curtain rising, difcovers the infide of a temple,
with an altar. Hymen enters, attended by boys
and girls bearing bafkets of flowers; fome drefs
the altar with garlands, and others ftrew the
ground.

HYMEN.

THIS day, my children, ufe diftinguifh'd care;
Let flow'ry trophies grace my facred fhrine;
With rofy garlands and frefh myrtle-wreaths

My

My altars deck, and round the vaulted aifles
Difperfe the fweeteft bloffoms of the fpring.
  Obedient to the dread command of Jove,
I from my native heav'n awhile defcend,
To grace the nuptials of a lovely pair,
On whofe aufpicious union fortune fmiles.

A I R.

  Flora, Goddefs of the fpring,
  Hafte, thy fweeteft treafure bring ;
  The dappled pink, the blufhing rofe,
  And ev'ry fragrant flow'r that blows,
  To fcent the air, and ftrew the way ;
  For this is ———'s nuptial day.

H Y M E N.

Ye gentle Zephyrs, on your balmy wings
Waft the rich odours which Arabia yields ;
And from Idume's fpicy vallies fan
Ambrofial breezes, gales of fweet perfume.
  Let lofty pæans rend the diftant fhores ;
The folemn organ and deep-founding lyre
With fofter lutes harmonioufly combine,
Till Albion's vales and rocky cliffs refound,
And hymeneal triumphs crown the day.

CHORUS.

CHORUS.

Sweep the founding lyre,
And ev'ry inftrument infpire,
Till echoing rocks return the found,
And foaming waves rebound,
Hymen triumphant reigns.

Breathe the warbling flute,
And gently ftrike the fofter lute;
'Till thro' the azure roofs on high
The fwelling notes reply,
Hymen triumphant reigns.

[*Minerva defcends.*

HYMEN.

Daughter of Jove, immortal Pallas, hail!

MINERVA.

Soft peace and everlafting pleafure wait
On holy Hymen, at whofe awful fhrine
By facred rites the lovers' vows are crown'd!
Bright as the fun thy torch fhall ever beam
In ——'s breaft with undiminifh'd ray.
'Tis not the voice of Fortune, but of Jove,
Confirms the doom ; for fhe, capricious Queen,
'Midft flow'ry paths conceals her fcorpion train,
And foothes with fmiles while fhe directs the dart:

But

But Jove, determin'd, steady, and sincere,
With gracious eye illustrious —— views,
Pleas'd with his virtues, with the glorious names
Patron of science and the Muse's friend.

From dark Obscurity's sequester'd shades,
Where Poverty, with cold and chilling hand,
Damps native genius, and restrains its flight,
Oft has he drawn the trembling Muse, and spread
Her infant pinions with the breath of praise;
Sooth'd all her fears, describ'd her devious way,
And bade her rise to fortune and to fame.

HYMEN.

Immortal blessings, such as love bestows,
When reason regulates the rising flame,
And friendship rivets the soft band he twines,
Such blessings shall await thy ——'s hours,
And soothe his soul with sweet domestic peace.

DUET.

HYMEN.

Soft peace and smiling pleasures wait
On love and friendship's blended flame,
Beyond the reach of envious Fate,
And guarded from her dang'rous aim.

D   Still

Still chearful as the ruddy morn,
No care the gentle union knows;
Selects the flower, but leaves the thorn,
And on the myrtle binds the rose.

MINERVA.

Serene thro' life's uncertain way,
May Fortune still great —— guide;
And, still array'd in smiles, display
Her banners o'er his happy bride!

Fair as the lilies of the spring,
In beauty gay and infant charms,
Latona, be the gifts you bring
To crown their hopes and bless their arms.

BOTH.

And still, as each intruding year
From either parent steals a grace,
Fresh may the rifled charms appear,
Reviving in their blooming race.

THE END OF THE FIRST ACT.

ACT

A C T THE S E C O N D.

The scene opening, discovers a vale with flocks
grazing, and a prospect of woods, mountains, and
corn-fields. Several nymphs enter, and erect a
triumphal arch of green boughs and garlands of
flowers.

A I R.

YE breezes who, in wanton play,
   Hover round the smiling May,
Lightly clad in vernal air,
Hither, hither all repair.

Come along, and in your way,
As thro' th' enamell'd meads ye stray,
Perfumes select from ev'ry flow'r,
To grace fair ———'s nuptial bow'r.

C H O R U S.

Hail! happy bridegroom, happy bride!
Britannia's hope, Britannia's pride!
For you the trophy'd arch we raise
Of roses and immortal bays.

For

For you the favouring God prepares
The joys of love without its cares;
On you his fweeteft fmiles attend;
On you his choiceft gifts defcend.

NYMPH.

Obedient to Minerva's foft command
The pageant rifes, and in rural pomp
Afcends triumphant o'er the flow'ry vale.
But fee, fhe comes !——   [*Minerva defcends.*
——————————— Immortal Pallas, hail !

MINERVA.

Not Enna's plains, where Proferpina rov'd
Ere gloomy Pluto feiz'd the trembling maid,
Or Ida's fhady brow (fweet haunt of Jove)
Can rival fair Britannia's beauteous vales,
Which Ceres, Flora, and Pomona grace.
  Here blufhing Spring her early revels keeps,
And here, defcending in foft vernal fhow'rs,
Spreads the gay bloffom, or with gentle hand
Unfolds the leafy honours of the grove;
Beneath whofe fhelt'ring canopy fhe rears
The primrofe pied, and lily's fnowy bell,
The purple violet, rich with fweet perfume,
And yellow cowflip fraught with balmy dew.

There

There level lawns diverſify the ſcene,
Where lowing oxen ſlowly move along,
(But lately loos'd from the laborious yoke)
And, bleſs'd with ſweet oblivion's healing wave,
Forget the paſt, nor dread the future goad ;
But ſtretch'd ſupine, inhale the balmy breeze,
Sr... the known ſpring, or crop the flow'ry food.
 There bleating flocks, freſh from the ſhearer's
  hand,
Bound o'er the lawn, and ſeek the ſunny hill,
Which caſts its lengthening ſhadow o'er the field.
 Here roſy nymphs, whoſe bluſhes ſhame the
  morn,
And ruddy youths, returning from the mead,
Healthy and innocent, the hamlet ſeek,
And gayly laugh, or chaunt the ruſtic ſong.
 And there in ſweet variety ariſe
Rich glebes deep furrow'd by the ploughman's toil,
Where bounteous Ceres, to reward their care,
With plenteous harveſt crowns the fertile plain.
 Pomona's bleſſings here adorn the boughs,
Thick as the cluſt'ring fruitage of the vine,
Which Phœbus tinges with a roſy hue,
More lovely than Heſperia's golden fruit.
 But Britain's glory and the choiceſt dow'r
Which Jove indulgent on her iſle beſtows,

Is

Is facred Liberty, that guards her throne,
And Freedom, whofe celeftial influence fires
With godlike virtue ev'ry gen'rous breaft
With fteady valour, to defend her laws
From Faction's turbulent unruly pow'r,
And balance juftice with impartial hand.

[The nymphs complete the arch.

NYMPH,

Immortal Queen! obedient to thy word,
With laurel garlands crown'd, and wreaths of flow'rs,
The finifh'd arch triumphantly appears.

MINERVA.

Your tafk accomplifh'd, thro' the yielding air
Awake fweet echo with harmonious fong,
Invoking Faunus and his fylvan train
To fhare the feftive mirth and fprightly dance.

CHORUS.

Fauns, who dwell on fhady mountains,
Nymphs, who rove near chryftal fountains,
Come away, come away.
Hark, the oaten reed's foft meafure,
Sweetly tun'd to love and pleafure,
Leads the dance, and we obey.

[A dance of nymphs.

AIR.

A I R.

Lur'd by mufic's magic pow'r,
See, they hafte from hill and grove;
Warbling fpring and fhady bower,
Soft retreats, fweet haunts of love.

Zephyr ftill, their way perfuming,
Steals the fweets of ev'ry dale;
Flora's gifts around them blooming,
Spread a carpet o'er the vale.
[*Faunus, &c. enter, and join the dance.*

C H O R U S.

Away, to the Temple of Hymen repair,
Where the Loves and the Virtues prefide,
Where Innocence reigns; for no Satyrs are there;
Where the bridegroom awaits the fair bride.

Away to the Temple of Hymen; away;
See the God waves his torch high in air;
The rites are prepar'd, and love chides our delay,
Then away, to the altar repair.

END OF THE SECOND ACT.

ACT

ACT THE THIRD.

HYMEN, MINERVA, &c.

MINERVA.

AVAUNT, each gloomy harbinger of care,
Intruding fighs, and melancholy tears;
Far from this hallow'd fcene your vigils keep,
Brood o'er the tomb, or feek the lonely cell
Where bigots mourn and fuperftition reigns.
Here, unappall'd by vifionary fears,
Let rofy pleafure fpread her varied wing,
And innocence, ftill chearful as the morn,
Array'd in fmiles, fit thron'd on ev'ry brow.

HYMEN.

Hail, happy day! aufpicious moment, hail!
Sacred to mirth and laughing joy ordain'd!
Still as the circling years awake thy dawn,
With bridal fplendor crown'd, may tranfports wake,
And new-born pleafures date their infant birth!
    May ev'ry blefling in the urn of Jove,
Unclouded by the bitter dregs of woe,
For ever flow around the wedded pair!
May downy peace and fweet content attend,
And fmoothe their paths, and guard their honour'd
    bow'r!   DUET.

D U E T.

HYMEN.

May pleafure ftill around them play,
And flowery be their future way;
And rifing honours, ever new,
Where'er they rove, their fteps purfue!

MINERVA.

In rofy bands, by Hymen twin'd,
May they unfading fragrance find;
And wreaths diffufing fweet perfume
Around their brows for ever bloom!

HYMEN.

Soft as the fhades of fetting day,
And tranquil, be their evening ray;
Nor time or hoary age impair
The joys which love and friendfhip fhare!

CHORUS.

The gentle yoke (foft chain) that binds
Twin hearts and fympathizing minds;
Which Heav'n approves, and reafon wears,
For them indulgent Fate prepares.

END OF THE MASK.

O D E

T O

H O P E,

I.

SWEET Hope, thou heav'n-born cherub ! why
From me regardlefs doft thou fly ?
Ah! why no more my lonely path illume?
Thy foothing voice, thy angel fmile,
Did oft my cares, my wrongs beguile,
And lead me fafe thro' wayward Fortune's gloom,

II.

But now abandon'd, fhun'd by thee,
I float on life's tempeftuous fea
A helplefs wreck, the fport of ev'ry tide.
Bewilder'd, loft, forlorn I ftray,
No beam to chear my weary way,
Or thro' the tracklefs path my fteps to guide.

III. Sifter

III.

Sifter of Faith ! once more defcend,
Not as a flatterer, but a friend,
And leave thy vifionary train behind :
Religion's tranquil mièn affume,
Fix all my views beyond the tomb,
And make me blefs'd, by making me refign'd.

ODE

O D E

T O

——————— ——————

I.

HE who to till the rugged foil
    Was by his humble birth defign'd,
Wou'd fhrink from the laborious toil,
    Had fcience form'd his early mind.

II.

The nervous arm, whofe ardent ftroke
    For Britain's navies oft employ'd,
Cou'd ne'er have fell'd the ftubborn oak,
    Had eafe its native ftrength deftroy'd.

III.

The foldier who, in hoftile climes,
    Extremes of cold and heat endures,
A hardy infancy betimes
    To every different change enures.

IV. But

IV.

But thou, whom favouring Fate endows
With inborn elegance of foul ;
With wealth that crowns thy utmoſt vows,
And bids no vulgar cares controul ;

V.

Shou'dſt range at large thro' ev'ry ſcene
Where poliſh'd taſte the heart refines ;
Where paſſions learn to flow ſerene,
And genius in full luſtre ſhines.

ODE

O D E

TO THE SAME.

I.

THINK not, my friend, impartial Fate
   By giddy chance directs her hand,
Tho' oft on knaves her favours wait,
Or bafe-born Flatt'ry's impious band.

II.

Riches are not the Hero's meed,
Or the infpiring Mufe's aim;
For them a nobler boon's decreed,
The laurels of immortal fame.

WRITTEN

[55]

WRITTEN IN 1777.

MY lute, my lyre, thrown carelefs by,
The oaten reed's wild notes I try;
And, leaving Pride's deluded train,
Ambition's haunts, and Folly's reign,
Of Flora's blufh and Zephyr's wing,
And rural beauties gayly fing.

See, in yonder eaftern fkies
The filver dawn falutes my eyes;
And waving woods and cloud-crown'd hills,
And fhadowy lawns and mifty rills,
Emerging faintly, meet the view,
Embath'd in tears of pearly dew.
The Lark, fweet harbinger of day,
Thro' æther wings his rapid way;
And as he floats the fkies along,
Pours the foft tribute of his fong.
And now from many a gorgeous fold
Of azure clouds enrich'd with gold,
The radiant God who rules the day
Chafes the lingering fhades away,

And

And in full luftre o'er the plain
Sheds the bright glories of his reign.
 Creation fmiles, the groves refound
With mufic's foft melodious found;
The plumy choir, the whifpering gale,
The rill flow murmuring thro' the vale,
In fweet according notes agree,
And breathe the foul of harmony.
 Now to the fields of ripen'd corn,
Waving with the breath of morn,
Ceres invites the rural band,
Each with his fickle in his hand;
While happinefs and rofy health,
The monarch's aim, the peafant's wealth,
Diffus'd thro' all the ruftic race,
Sparkle and glow in ev'ry face.
 To fhare the gifts of Ceres' reign,
The hamlet fends its blooming train;
And ev'ry lafs, elate, prepares
To feek and bind the fcatter'd ears;
Ranging at large around the plain,
Or loitering near fome favourite fwain.
 Now toil affumes the face of joy;
The youths their manly ftrength employ,
More chearful while the laugh goes round,
Or fongs of fprightly nymphs refound:

And

And as their labours thus advance,
Full many a tender fide-long glance
Each lover fteals, and flyly leaves
Some ftraggling ftalks from plenteous fheaves,
To crown the darling gleaner's toil,
And win from her a partial fmile;
While fhe, unconfcious of a thought
With bafe diffimulation fraught,
His fond attention fweetly feels,
And blufhing, all her foul reveals:
For love (in courts an empty name)
Is here a mutual generous flame,
That glowing friendfhip of the heart
Which fcorns referve, difguife, or art.

Now the fultry noon-tide hour
Invites to yonder upland bow'r,
Where a cool fpring, o'er-arch'd with trees,
Gives frefhnefs to the languid breeze.
There (with robes unzon'd) fupine
I'll on the velvet mofs recline,
From life and all its cares retir'd;
And, by the Mufe alone infpir'd,
I'll fing the beauties of the fhade,
The landfcape opening to the glade,
The flocks that range the flow'ry vale,

E

The

The fragrance of the balmy gale,
The groves of variegated green,
The rill meandering thro' the scene,
The lake with silver bosom spread,
The mouldering tow'r, the straw-roof'd shed,
The distant spires that pierce the skies,
The mountains that still bolder rise,
Whose white rocks o'er the forest show
Like fleecy clouds or drifted snow.

　There too, in sable weeds array'd,
Sweet Melancholy, pensive maid,
Shall teach the tender tear to flow
In all the luxury of woe;
While Petrarch mourns o'er Laura's tomb,
Or Lyttelton his Lucy's doom;
Or make those softer sorrows mine
Which thrill thro' Hammond's polish'd line.

　Or, led by the historic Muse,
Her fair recording page peruse;
With mind unbias'd and serene,
Impartial scan each human scene;
Trace fierce Rebellion to its source,
And mark the Tyrant's blood-stain'd course;
Observe how Discord rules the ball;
How factions rise, how empires fall;

How

How Vice uplifts her crefted head;
How Pride, with eagle-pinions fpread,
Now towers, now ftoops at Fortune's lure,
A fhort-liv'd glory to enfure:
How bold Ambition ftalks around,
Deform'd with many a ghaftly wound;
His heart againft compaffion fteel'd,
His fpear high rais'd, which fcorns to yield,
Tho' Honour checks, tho' Mercy pleads,
And Juftice midft his triumphs bleeds.
How mifers brood with greedy eye,
O'er hoarded wealth they won't enjoy;
For years remote vaft fchemes defign,
And midft abounding plenty pine.

Are thefe the paths which lead to fame?
Can guilt deferve the Hero's name?
Will Confcience, lull'd, ferenely reft
Beneath a conqueror's waving creft,
Tho' every plume was rudely tore
From Virtue's brow, and drench'd in gore?
Will fweet Content, will Peace defcend,
Tho' coffers fwell, tho' lands extend?
Will Death his deftin'd victim lofe,
If pale decrepit Av'rice fues?

E 3   When

When the fierce bolt of angry Jove
Flies wing'd with vengeance from above,
'Tis not the breath of vain applaufe
Can then fupport a guilty caufe.
'Tis not the fplendid crowds that wait
To fwell the empty pomp of ftate,
Can guard you, in that awful hour,
From Juftice' dread offended pow'r.
'Tis not amidft thofe blooming groves
Where loofe-rob'd Pleafure carelefs roves;
Where Mufic tunes her fofteft lay,
And melts the lift'ning foul away;
That Heaven will hear a guilty vow,
Or Vice conceal her impious brow.
    'Tis not th' accumulated ftore
Of fparkling gems and burnifh'd ore,
Can a remorfe-ftung mind appeafe,
Or give to Fraud a tranfient eafe,
When to the dreadful verge he's come
Of dark eternity, whofe gloom
Virtue herfelf with awe beholds,
Tho' Hope her radiant wings unfolds.
    Deluded mortals! learn to know
The fource whence genuine blifs muft flow.
Within your reach the boon is plac'd;
Its paths for every fphere are trac'd.

Truft

Truſt Reaſon—ſhe'll ſecurely guide
Your way thro' life's tempeſtuous tide;
Will each unruly paſſion tame,
And bend them to a nobler aim.
Ambition, temper'd by her hand,
Shall firſt amidſt the Virtues ſtand;
By her his ſavage fierceneſs tam'd,
His brutal ſtrength, his rage reclaim'd,
No more ſhall build unjuſt applauſe
On Nature's violated laws;
Nor pow'r uſurp'd, nor guilt-ſtain'd fame,
Debaſe the Hero's glorious name.
Ev'n Avarice, his brow unbent,
Shall learn the leſſon of content:
No more his niggard hand refuſe
An alms when weeping Miſery ſues,
Or his inhoſpitable dome
Command an exil'd ſon to roam.
Love too, which gracious Heav'n deſign'd
To harmonize the yielding mind,
By Innocence and Reaſon led,
Shall her diffuſive influence ſhed,
To ſweeten all the dregs of woe,
And bid our cup with bleſſings flow.

E 3   Theſe

These are the tasks to thee assign'd,
Thou tamer of the human mind,
Immortal Reason!—thy controul
Distinguishes the Heav'n-born soul;
Gives it its origin to know,
The source from whence its virtues flow:
Gives it ambition to aspire
Beyond each grov'ling base desire;
And wing'd by Hope to rise beyond the tomb,
Fresh with immortal life, and never-fading bloom.

ODE

O D E

TO

FRIENDSHIP.

I.

FOND Love, with all his winning wiles
   Of tender looks and flattering smiles;
Of accents that might Juno charm,
Or Dian's colder ear alarm;
No more shall play the tyrant's part,
No more shall lord it o'er my heart.

II.

To Friendship (sweet benignant Power!)
I consecrate my humble bower,
My lute, my muse, my willing mind,
And fix her in my heart enshrin'd:
She, Heaven-descended Queen! shall be
My tutelar Divinity.

III. Soft

III.

Soft Peace defcends to guard her reign
From anxious fear and jealous pain :
She no delufive hopes difplays,
But calmly guides our tranquil days ;
Refines our pleafure, foothes our care,
And gives the joys of Eden here.

SONG.

S O N G.

ON a bank young Thyrfis lay,
   Blooming as the God of day:
The flow'rs he prefs'd feem'd pleas'd to hide
Beneath his form their blufhing pride.

The breezy Zephyrs fporting there,
Fann'd with their wings the dewy air,
While Morpheus, hov'ring round his head,
Gentle flumbers foftly fhed.

ODE.

O D E.

I.

FOR different ranks and different minds
   Diſtinct purſuits juſt Fate decrees;
For thoſe the laurel garland binds,
The prize of ſcience twines for theſe.

II.

The Muſe alone at large may range,
Her free-born ſpirit ſcorns controul:
Tho' nations fall, tho' empires change,
Her lyre reſounds from pole to pole.

III.

One artiſt bids the marble breathe,
And * Howe's firm ſoul the buſt inſpires;
Another wins the envy'd wreath,
While † Wolfe in glowing tincts expires.

* Lord Howe, who was unfortunately killed in America, laſt war.

† General Wolfe, whoſe death at the ſiege of Quebec is ſo finely painted by Mr. Weſt.

IV. Great

IV.

Great thefe attempts, and juft their praife,
To build the Hero's bright renown;
Fortune beftows, they paint the bays,
But ftill the Mufe muft fix the crown.

V.

Her facred page records their deeds;
Her golden pencil ftamps their fame:
Still in her fong brave * Ruffell bleeds,
And † Ca'ndifh boafts a patriot's name.

---

* William Lord Ruffell, beheaded in the reign of Charles the Second.

† William Earl (afterwards Duke) of Devonfhire, who had a principal fhare in the Revolution.

O D E

TO

V E N U S.

I.

WHAT mean thefe tumults in my breaft,
    This tender figh, this trickling tear,
This tranfient joy by grief fupprefs'd,
This flatt'ring hope chaftiz'd by fear?

II.

Why, fhun'd by every fprightly Mufe,
To foft complaints attune my lyre?
Why focial fcenes no longer chufe,
But ftill to lonely groves retire?

III.

Ha, Love! 'tis thy intruding dart!
I feel, I feel the kindling flame:
Thou rul'ft the empire of my heart,
Difguis'd in Friendfhip's fpecious name.

IV. Fair

IV.

Fair Venus ! to thy pow'r I bow,
To thee prefer my humble fuit ;
With myrtle garlands bind my brow,
With rofes crown my votive lute !

V.

Indulgent Queen of foft defire,
Oh view me proftrate at thy fane !
Why doft thou thus my foul infpire ?
Why bid me wear a ufelefs chain ?

VI.

If foft compaffion's gentle plea
E'er ftole perfuafive on thy mind,
As Damon's heart let mine be free,
Or both in flowery fetters bind !

VII.

Or, to the cares of love decreed,
Let Damon in his turn complain ;
Unpity'd mourn, unheeded plead,
To me, regardlefs of his pain !

VIII.

Ah, no ! avert the guilty pray'r—
Love fix'd as mine can never ftray ;
Or flights, or circling years impair
The flame illum'd by Friendfhip's ray.

IX. In

IX.

In gloomy caves, or leaflefs bowers,
While I my lonely moments lead,
May Pleafure crown his happier hours,
Fair Friendfhip's joys, and Virtue's meed!

O D E

TO

V E N U S.

I.

OH Cyprian Queen! whose praise I sing,
  Whose willing vot'ry I remain,
Teach me to touch the Teian string,
And swell the love-commanding strain!

II.

Descending oft to Sappho's pray'r,
Thy turtles sought the Lesbian shade;
Their wings perfum'd the yielding air,
Their murmurs sooth'd the love-lorn maid.

III.

Nor less indulgent to my suit,
Wilt thou, immortal Venus! prove;
Tho' rude my voice and artless lute,
Yet pity pleads the cause of love.

IV.

Come then, propitious Goddess! come,
Oh give my Damon to my arms!
Regardless he'll no longer roam,
When thou shalt aid the Muse's charms.

A BAL-

A

B A L L A D,

WRITTEN IN JUNE, 1775.

I.

YE fubjeâts of Britain, attend to my fong;
    For, to you both the Mufe and her numbers
      belong:
No courtier, no hireling, no penfioner fhe;
By int'reft unfway'd, and from prejudice free.

II.

A fubjeât I chufe for the theme of my lays,
Well known to this realm in Elizabeth's days;
That period of glory, that age of renown,
When a female fupported the rights of the crown.

III.

A Cabal there was form'd by the foes of the ftate,
Who like —— and —— could in fenate debate:
Foreign gold lin'd their pockets, and bulls·from the
    Pope
Remov'd all reftraint, and gave confcience full fcope.

IV. With

IV.

With manners and morals adapted to pleafe,
'They flow'd with opinions, as waves with the
 breeze ;
For Rome grants indulgence for aiding her caufe,
And, to favour her int'reft, relaxes her laws.

V.

Well vers'd in diffembling, 'midft Jefuits bred,
And deep in each lecture of Machiavel read ;
With a latitude Truth muft for ever deteft,
They cenfur'd the tenets their hearts ftill profefs'd ;

VI.

And loudly exclaim'd, that the nation again
Wou'd fink to the level of Mary's weak reign ;
For that Burleigh, and thofe at the head of
 affairs,
From the cries of her people, had turn'd the Queen's
 ears :

VII.

That a debt juftly due to the Spaniards (they faid)
Thro' the bafeft mifmanagement, ftill lay unpaid :
That Iberia was arming her right to demand,
And had mann'd a huge fleet, which no pow'r cou'd
 withftand :

F   VIII. That

VIII.

That myriads of treafure, and oceans of gore,
Was the int'reft we foon with the loan muft reftore;
And that nought cou'd avert it, or ward off the
　　blow,
But the Miniftry's ruin and fwift overthrow.

IX.

Thus, with idle chimeras the people amus'd,
Their judgment perverted, their reafon abus'd,
Obnoxious alike ev'ry ftatefman appear'd :
They were cenfur'd, revil'd, and condemn'd tho'
　　unheard.

X.

For Prejudice fuffers not Juftice to fway ;
Caprice is the law that her fubjects obey;
And the culprit is either accus'd or commended,
Not for what he has done, but what party offended.

XI.

This point once attain'd, and the popular name
Of Patriot affum'd, to eftablifh their fame,
They laugh'd at thofe gudgeons who fwallow'd the
　　bait,
And plann'd (in its guardians) the fall of the ftate.

XII. For

XII.

For they knew them fo firm, fo attach'd to the laws,
To religion, to truth, and Elizabeth's caufe,
That, ere they cou'd give thefe a final o'erthrow,
They firft at their bofoms muft level the blow.

XIII.

So away to Whitehall they determin'd to hie them,
And fee if her Majefty dar'd to deny them,
When they fhou'd demand the immediate difgrace
Of friends, fav'rites, minifters—all thofe in place.

XIV.

Arriv'd at the palace, they foon gain'd admiffion,
As due to their rank, not their vaunted commiffion;
And boldly advanc'd to the foot of the throne,
Pretended abufes and wrongs to make known.

XV.

The Queen, with a placid but refolute eye,
Prepar'd for a kind or an angry reply,
As their ftile might deferve; moft attentively heard
    them,
And fhew'd that fhe neither neglected nor fear'd them.

XVI.

With eloquence fram'd, their deep arts to difguife,
To fafcinate reafon by fudden furprize,
To lull the found judgment to drowfy repofe,
And win and infinuate ftill as it flows;

F 2   XVII. They

XVII.

They talk'd of abuses, of rights unprotected,
Of the wrongs we endur'd, and of those we expected;
And, swell'd with importance, began to arraign
A conduct too partial, which made them complain.

XVIII.

Said, our freedom hung pois'd in a wavering scale;
That the opposite balance must shortly prevail:
For they knew by that charm they shou'd strengthen
 the spell,
Which alone cou'd the schemes they concerted
 conceal.

XIX.

But the Queen's penetration detected the snare;
No soft flowing words cou'd impose on her ear:
Yet, wisely dissembling, she mildly desir'd
They'd freely declare all her people requir'd.

XX.

Encourag'd by this, opportunely they thought
The ministry's fall might be easily wrought;
And began to complain of their overgrown pow'r,
Which our freedom, our wealth, and our laws wou'd
 devour.

XXI. Said,

XXI.

Said, their meafures were wrong, and their admini-
 ftration
Obnoxious alike to all ranks in the nation;
Their difgrace they muft therefore moft humbly
 advife,
Left the chiefs fhould revolt and the populace rife.

XXII.

Unmov'd by the menace, Elizabeth frown'd
So fternly, as might the moft daring confound;
And, enrag'd at their pride, ftruck the globe with
 her hand,
That enfign of honour and regal command.

XXIII.

" By the God that I worfhip (if rightly I ween)
" They're my friends, and I've prov'd them," reply'd
 the fair Queen;
" As fuch I regard them, as fuch I'll defend;
" So defift from complaining, and to me attend.

XXIV.

" As long as the fcepter of Britain I fway,
" I'll rule like a Queen, and ye all fhall obey:
" No laws I'll infringe, and no infolent Peer
" Shall prefume to intrude on the Royal barrier.

F 3   XXV. " My

XXV.

" My fervants I'll chufe, and my friends I'll reward;
" To the good of my fubjects fhew proper regard :
" But when traitors the peace of my crown would
" deftroy,
" Let Juftice the fword of correction employ.

XXVI.

Repuls'd and abafh'd, from the throne they retir'd,
And ne'er, from that moment, 'gainft ftatefmen
confpir'd,
Whofe wifdom and virtue fecur'd them efteem,
And ftill furnifh the Mufe with a favourite theme.

XXVII.

Succefs crown'd the meafures they wifely purfu'd ;
Our friendfhip was courted, our treaties renew'd,
Our commerce extended; while peace reign'd at
home,
And Britain fhook off the laft fhackle of Rome.

T W O

TWO ELEGIES.

ARGUMENT.

In the two following Elegies, Chriſtina Queen of
Sweden is repreſented bewailing the tyranny of
Cuſtom, and the reſtraint ſhe was under with reſpect to Marriage; and at length determining to
ſacrifice her intereſt to her love, by abdicating a
crown which ſhe was not permitted to ſhare with
her lover.

ELEGY THE FIRST.

I.

THOU tyrant Cuſtom! whoſe relentleſs laws
   Nature and Juſtice ſtill oppoſe in vain;
Will no kind angel plead my injur'd cauſe?
Will no avenging arm deſtroy thy chain?

II.

Muſt Love (that gentle Pow'r, whoſe ſoft'ning ſmiles
The ſavage fierceneſs of Revenge can tame,
Or ſoothe Ambition with perſuaſive wiles,
And lure him back from the purſuits of fame);

III.

Muſt he, low bending to thy ſtern command,
The roſy garland and the bow reſign;
In courts a mean neglected captive ſtand,
And by thy laws his juſter ſway confine?

IV.

No, abject ſhade! let thy imagin'd hand
O'er coward minds the iron ſceptre wield;
A ſoul ſuperior ſpurns thy baſe command,
And bids thy rules to Reaſon's dictates yield.

V.

From regal pomp and regal cares retir'd,
I'll loſe the ſov'reign in a ſofter name;
By fools condemn'd, but by the brave admir'd,
And crown'd at once with happineſs and fame.

ELEGY

ELEGY THE SECOND.

CHRISTINA to ALEXIS.

I.

NOT great Guſtavus his exalted throne,
   His fair dominions, or his wealth, I prize;
To bear the toils of royalty alone,
Or ſee ſome monarch by my favour riſe.

II.

Tho' Fortune ſmiles on my auſpicious reign,
Since Fate forbids that thou ſhou'dſt ſhare the dow'r,
For thee the pomp of empire I'll diſdain,
And all the high-plum'd pageantry of pow'r.

III.

A ſoul like mine cou'd well ſuch trappings ſpare:
But ſay, wilt thou renounce Ambition's aim
For me? the withering breath of Cenſure dare,
And ſpurn the civic wreath, the hero's proud
   acclaim?

IV. Wilt

IV.

Wilt thou, like me, for fome fequefter'd fhade,
Some village cot, thefe ftately domes refign,
Where Wealth, where Fame, where Pride muft
　　ne'er invade,
But all be facrific'd at Friendfhip's fhrine?

V.

Love fhuns the troubled haunts of pomp and noife;
Clofe in a myrtle grove his temple ftands;
There he diffufes all his pureft joys,
And binds uniting hearts in flow'ry bands.

VI.

But Cupid fcorns to hold divided fway,
Nor with Ambition deigns to fhare a throne;
Who owns his fceptre muft his will obey,
And bend to him, defpotic Pow'r! alone.

VII.

If then Alexis loves, he'll lead the way
Thro' Ruffian deferts or th' Atlantic wave,
Rather than here 'midft taftelefs fplendor ftay,
The dupe of Folly, and vain Fortune's flave.

THE

SYLPH LOVER.

A SONG.

I.

HERE in this fragrant bower I dwell,
    And nightly here repofe;
My couch a lily's fnowy bell,
My canopy a rofe.
The honey-dew each morn I fip,
That hangs upon the violet's lip;
And, like the bee, from flower to flower
I carelefs rove at noon-tide hour.

II.

Regardlefs as I lately ftray'd
Along the myrtle grove,
Enchanting mufic round me play'd,
Soft as the voice of love.
Thus its fweet murmurs feem'd to fay,
" Fond, thoughtlefs wanton, come away!
" For while you rove, a rival's charms
" Win thy Myrtilla to his arms."

ELEGY.

E L E G Y.

WRITTEN IN A CONVENT.

WRETCH that I am! what fate averts my
 doom,
And bars my way to the fequefter'd tomb,
Where foft Oblivion drowns our vain defires;
Where hopelefs Love's confuming flame expires;
Where Mifery fleeps, where Sorrow finds repofe,
And the laft fcenes of Life's dark drama clofe?

Death, partial tyrant! whofe mifguided fpear
The happy wifh to fhun, the guilty fear;
Why, loit'ring ftill on Time's uncertain wing,
Muft diftant age thy flow approaches bring,
When the afflicted foul implores thy fpeed,
And courts the blow, impatient to be freed?
Oft uninvok'd, 'midft Fortune's favour'd train,
Where Love, and Joy, and gay Contentment reign,
Thy

Thy haggard band of pale difeafes fly,
Chill the warm heart, and dim the fparkling eye;
Or, ftill unaw'd, impetuous force their way,
Where Pomp and Wealth their pageant glare difplay;
Where wanton Luxury each art refines,
And pamper'd Pow'r on ftately thrones reclines;
Where proud Ambition boafts her daring claim,
And builds her aerie in the heights of fame.
Still there thy ruthlefs dart in fecret wounds,
And in one fate their lofty aims confounds:
But from the mournful call of plaintive woe,
Whofe pulfe fcarce beats, whofe blood forgets to
    flow,
From drooping fpirits, by afflidion broke,
Thou fly'ft regardlefs, and delay'ft the ftroke.

Where then can I, poor love-lorn maid, appeal,
Where hope for refuge from the wrongs I feel,
Since Death, whofe arm alone could bring relief,
Smiles at my anguifh, and infults my grief?

Here in thefe hallow'd domes, thefe facred fhades,
Where heav'n-born Peace her filver pinions fpreads;
Where calm Religion lends her tranquil ray,
Illumes the path, and points the glorious way;
For me no beam of holy grace defcends;
For me no Hope her balmy wing extends:

                                        But

2

But Love directs the figh Repentance claims,
And reigns triumphant, tho' Reflection blames.

From reftlefs flumbers and tumultuous dreams
Of long-loft pleafures or delufive fchemes,
Wak'd by the midnight bell, to pray'r I rife,
Guilt in my heart and terror in my eyes,
And thro' the vaulted aifles reluctant move,
With feign'd devotion, tho' the flave of Love.
O'er holy martyrs' fculptur'd tombs I tread,
Where beaming glories mark the fainted head ;
Where virgins live in monumental brafs,
And feem to chide as I, frail fifter! pafs ;
But chide in vain—regardlefs of their frown,
Love flights the gilded fhrine, the ftarry crown ;
His impious fway the guilty Pow'r maintains,
Throbs in my heart, and thrills thro' all my veins.

Now proftrate at the altar's foot I bow,
Bewail my errors, and renew my vow,
Implore for mercy, which I yet abufe,
And plead for grace, tho' I that grace refufe ;
While fault'ring accents ftill confefs the pray'r
Not by Religion form'd, but by Defpair ;
And wandering thoughts, and a rebellious heart,
Renounce that peace repentance would impart.

The

The nightly hymn and folemn fervice o'er,
Trembling, my lonely cloifter I explore;
And there (while round me, funk in foft repofe,
Each fhares the fweet oblivion fleep beftows,
While yet no prieft, no lift'ning veftal hears)
I feize the moment facred to my tears;
Give a full loofe to anguifh and defpair,
And breathe my forrows to the vacant air.

Then, if exhaufted Nature feeks repofe,
And tranfient flumbers my fad eye-lids clofe,
Fancy, ftill free, the magic drama forms;
Replete with foaming waves and threat'ning ftorms,
Methinks Alonzo rides the angry main,
And fpurns me (finking) while I plead in vain;
Or with his arms the furious furge divides,
And bears fome happier rival o'er the tides;
While plung'd at once beneath the whelming flood,
Dim grow my eyes, and cold the circling blood,
As fome wide-gaping chafm or gloomy cave
Receives me fainting, and affords a grave.

Or, fhould more pleafing objects form the fcene,
A beauteous landfcape and a heav'n ferene,
Sicilia's vales and Cyprus' blooming groves,
Haunt of the Graces and the infant Loves;
Yet there Alonzo's form falutes my view,
And flies unkindly, while I ftill purfue:

10   Tho'

Tho' tangling grafs and flow'rs perverfely meet,
Impede my way, and catch my ftruggling feet.
  Or if awhile fome fond delufion charms,
And brings this vagrant lover to my arms,
Religion, frowning, the fhort joy denies,
And tears the fweet enchantment from my eyes.
The matin bell bids all its beauties fade,
The rofy bow'rs, and my Alonzo's fhade.
Yet on the mind fuch flatt'ring traits they leave,
Again I flumber, and again believe:
Alonzo all his former vows renews;
He fighs, he pleads, till every doubt I lofe;
Then fweetly fmiling feems to chide my ftay,
Unfolds the ponderous gates, and leads the way.
But foon the bell's repeated found I hear;
The vifion flies, refolv'd to empty air—
I rife, and wrapt within the fhelt'ring veil,
Weep o'er my forrows, and my vows bewail;
But weep in vain, in thofe lone cells immur'd,
By laws devoted, and by walls fecur'd;
Watch'd by pale fifters, who my tears arraign,
And e'en refufe the freedom to complain.
Unpity'd captive! where can I appeal;
To whom my forrows or my wrongs reveal;
Deny'd the privilege Affliction claims,
Which Heav'n allows, tho' harfh Religion blames?
                              A SONG.

A S O N G.

I.

OH Corydon, where doſt thou ſtray?
  To what far diſtant clime art thou flown,
Where Fame ne'er extended her ſway,
Where the Muſe and her lute are unknown?

II.

Are the nymphs of thoſe vallies more fair?
Are the charms they poſſeſs more divine?
Ah! inconſtant! how oft didſt thou ſwear,
That no beauty cou'd pleaſe thee but mine!

III.

Fond fool that I was, to believe
Such language cou'd never beguile!
That vows were not made to deceive,
Or falſhood to lurk in a ſmile!

IV.

Oh Memory! why the ſoft ſcene
Of our loves doſt thou ever renew?
Oh why ſtill in vain o'er the green
Do my eyes a falſe rover purſue?

G   V. Oblivion,

V.

Oblivion! sweet balm of our woes,
Where, where thy calm spring may I find?
Its wave shall restore my repose,
And banish his form from my mind.

VI.

Ah no! thus engrav'd on my heart,
What charm can his image remove?
That will ne'er be erased by art,
Which was drawn by the pencil of Love.

JENNY'S

JENNY's FAREWELL
TO
PETIE.

I.

WITH ſtreaming eyes and aching heart,
  Poor Jenny ſaw the flag diſplay'd;
And muſt we, Petie, muſt we part?
And wilt thou leave thy Jane? ſhe ſaid.

II.

Oh, if my Petie lov'd ſo true,
Not thus from my fond arms he'd ſtray,
A fleeting ſhadow to purſue,
Or a deluſive voice obey.

III.

What is the wavering breath of Fame,
Or what Profuſion's gaudy glare?
A phantom, an ideal name,
Mere ſcenery of painted air.

IV. Let

IV.

Let Folly bafk in Fortune's fmiles,
And idly court her fleeting joys ;
We'll fhun the fair, the flatt'ring wiles,
Since Love difdains her ufelefs toys.

V.

Back to the Highlands let us go,
And leave Ambition far behind ;
There fancy'd fpring 'midft fnows fhall glow,
And mufic float on ev'ry wind.

VI.

Fond love fhall gild each dreary fcene,
And teach our native rocks to bloom ;
Clothe bleakeft wilds in lively green,
And breathe from heath-grown hills perfume.

VII.

What are Idume's fragrant gales,
Tho' with ten thoufand odours fraught,
When ev'ry fenfe of pleafure fails,
And diftant flies each penfive thought ?

VIII.

Not fylvan fcenes or vernal charms
Can Jenny's fick'ning fancy pleafe,
If Petie wanders from her arms,
The fport of ruthlefs winds and feas.

IX. Oh

IX.

Oh wilt thou then unkindly rove
Thro' joys thy laſſie muſt not ſhare;
Forget thy vows of faithful love,
And baſely court ſome wealthier fair

X.

Forbid it, all ye ſacred Powers
Who ſmil'd upon our mutual flame,
When ſoft as dews, or April ſhow'rs,
Love ſtole on Friendſhip's colder name !

XI.

Her accents fail'd, but ſtill her ſighs
More eloquent than language plead ;
Nor leſs perſuaſive ſpeak her eyes,
While tears to falling tears ſucceed.

XII.

The youth now half relenting ſtood,
And oft her cheek with kiſſes preſt,
And oft his tender vows renew'd,
Tho' ſighs the fault'ring ſounds repreſs'd.

XIII.

The rougher paſſions all gave way,
And love had triumph'd o'er his heart,
Wou'd time have deign'd a tranſient ſtay;
But Heav'n decreed that they muſt part.

G 3   XIV. And

XIV.

And now the drum beat loud alarms;
His comrades all appear'd in view:
He burſt from her encircling arms,
Nor waited for one fond adieu.

SONG.

S O N G.

I.

THO' Love and each harmonious Maid
    To gentle Sappho lent their aid,
Yet, deaf to her enchanting tongue,
Proud Phaon fcorn'd her melting fong.

II.

Miftaken nymph ! hadft thou ador'd
Fair Fortune, and her fmiles implor'd;
Had fhe indulgent own'd thy claim,
And given thee wealth inftead of fame,

III.

Tho' harfh thy voice, deform'd and old,
Yet fuch th' omnipotence of gold,
The youth had foon confefs'd thy charms,
And flown impatient to thy arms.

THE

THE

P R U D E,

A

C O M I C   O P E R A.

The Author hopes her readers will be fo indulgent, as to confi-
der that this Opera was intended for the ftage, and moft of the
airs compofed for particular tunes. This apology fhe thought
it neceffary to make, as the meafure of fome of them might
otherwife have appeared fingular.

PERSONS of the DRAMA.

MEN.

EARL OF LEWINGTON, *disguised as a Peasant, in love with* Clementina.

SIR WILLIAM SANDBY, *his Friend, in love with* Jenny.

DON PEDRO DE MENDOZA, *Father to* Clementina.

FATHER DOMINICK, *an artful Priest.*

ROGER, *a Villager, in love with* Jenny.

WOMEN.

CLEMENTINA, *in love with the* Earl of Lewington, *but intended by her Father for a Nun.*

GRIZILDA, *Sister to* Don Pedro.

JENNY, *in love with* Sir William Sandby, *who she imagines a Peasant.*

MRS. WILSON, *supposed Mother to* Jenny.

SCENE a Village, &c. in a remote part of *England.*

Time of action twelve hours.

THE

P R U D E,

A

COMIC OPERA.

ACT the FIRST.

Scene a caftle, with a meadow before it: on one
fide, a grove, and on the other, a profpect of the
adjacent country. Clementina and Jenny are dif-
covered feated on a bank at the foot of a tree; the
former playing on a lute.

AIR the FIRST.

ADORN'D with the beauties of May,
  Here nature luxuriant is feen;
Sweet flowers in blooming array
Enamel the fmooth-fhaven green.

From

From the banks of yon murmuring rill,
Where the vi'let fpontaneoufly fprings,
Frefh odours the breezes exhale,
And wantonly waft on their wings.

The wood-lark's wild notes fill the grove,
While the finch warbles fweet on the fpray;
They tune their foft carols to love,
And hail the approaches of May.

But harfh founds their mufic to me,
Severely condemn'd in my bloom
A convent's ftrict rules to obey,
And pine in a monaft'ry's gloom.

CLEMENTINA.

Oh Jenny! how unfortunate am I! Condemn'd
to wafte the gay meridian of youth in the dark receffes of a lonely cell; and leave the world and all
its innocent pleafures, at the very moment when
my heart languifhes to enjoy them.

JENNY.

Are you really determin'd to obey your father,
and take the veil?

CLEMENTINA.

How can I avoid it?

JENNY.

JENNY.

No parent in the univerfe fhou'd force me into a convent againft my confent.

CLEMENTINA.

You talk extravagantly, my dear :—but, pray what wou'd you do, if you was in my fituation ?

JENNY.

Leave my father to fhew his zeal for religion in fome other manner, and feek liberty where I cou'd find it.

CLEMENTINA.

You would not furely forget the duty that is due to a parent, and follow your own inclination ?

JENNY.

Indeed I fhou'd, rather than fubmit to be a nun.

AIR THE SECOND.

Wild with furprize, with fear oppreft,
The new-fledg'd bird forfakes its neft,
And flutt'ring, feeks fome diftant tree,
If boys invade its liberty.
Dear liberty, fweet liberty, &c.

To

To deferts drear, and woods unknown,
The coward hind will bound alone,
Rather than wait the toils, and be
Confin'd, and lofe fweet liberty, &c.

Shall we, my friend, lefs wife than they,
Still loiter on the dang'rous way?
No—free as air, as fancy free,
We'll fly, and feek fweet liberty, &c.

CLEMENTINA.

Alas! where can I fly?—who will grant an afy-
lum to a friendlefs runaway?

JENNY.

Is there no kind friend, no generous lover, in
whofe arms you may find protection from the cru-
elty of an infatuated father?

CLEMENTINA.

Heigh-ho!————

JENNY.

Ha, Clementina! that heart-felt figh betrays a
fecret I have never been acquainted with.

CLEMENTINA.

It is the only circumftance of my·life I ever conceal'd from you. 'Twas delicacy, not diftruft, that

3   occafion'd

occafion'd my filence. I often wifh'd to converfe with you upon a theme which continually employs my thoughts; but I did not know how to introduce it. That difficulty is now remov'd; and I will own to you, 'tis love (that cruel deftroyer of repofe) which triumphs over every filial duty, and makes me fhudder at the thoughts of a veil.

AIR THE THIRD.

May you with Friendfhip's healing balm
Affuage the anguifh of my heart;
Charm the rude tempeft to a calm,
Or in my forrows bear a part!

JENNY.

Hufh, hufh! yonder comes Father Dominick and your aunt. Suppofe we retire into the grove, before they obferve us, and avoid being interrupted by them.

CLEMENTINA.

With all my heart.   [Exeunt.

Enter FATHER DOMINICK and GRIZILDA.

GRIZILDA.

Oh, Father Dominick! Father Dominick! what a bleffed thing it is to fee the church profper fo! if

                                        our

our pious Queen Mary survives but a few years
longer, there will be nothing but sanctity in the
nation. Not long ago, it was shameful to behold
the young huffies staring the fellows in the face, at
all their profane affemblies; but now, by our Lady,
it does one's heart good to see how the nunneries are
crowded!—and they say her Majefty (Heaven profper her) is determined to burn all the Heretics,
and endow monafteries with their eftates.

FATHER DOMINICK.

God fpare her, to execute her righteous intention!
So fare thee well, Grizilda. I muft depart, for I
have three nunneries to confefs ere noon.

DUET the FOURTH.

GRIZILDA.

Ha, Dominick! I fear
Thy greateft bufinefs there
Is not as a prieft, but a lover.
But by the Mafs I fwear,
If the nuns are all thy care,
The plot thou haft laid I'll difcover.

FATHER

FATHER DOMINICK.

Pſha! caſt thy fears away;
Doſt think ſuch chits as they
Can rival thy prudence and merit?
The Spaniard to beguile,
We muſt wear the maſk a while,
And then we'll his fortune inherit.

GRIZILDA.

Well, God ſpeed thee, Dominick! and remember
thou art ſworn to make me the wife of thy boſom,
as ſoon as the fortune is thine, and thou haſt ob-
tained a diſpenſation to marry. [*Exit.*

Manet FATHER DOMINICK.

What a fool do I make of this old amorous dotard! Doth ſhe think, that when I am in poſſeſſion
of her brother Don Pedro's riches, I'll wed ſuch a
piece of ſuperannuated mortality as ſhe is? No, no,
Grizil; when once Clementina is cloiſter'd, and I
have accompliſh'd my deſign, I'll ſhake thee off,
like an old caſſock not worth the wearing. — Now,
let me ſee :— [*taking a paper out of his boſom.*] This
is a copy of Don Pedro's will—would it was per-
fected, and he in the tomb with Saint Alban! *he
reads*] " I bequeath to the Nunnery of Saint Cathe-
" rine of bleſſed memory, 200 crowns *per annum*,
" for the maintenance of my dear daughter Cle-

H " mentina."

" mentina."—The Abbefs and I fhall go halves there. [*he reads again.*] " *Item.* I bequeath to the Chapel " of our Lady at Loretto, 800 crowns." That finks here—[*fhaking his pocket.*] " And laftly, I will and " defire, that the refidue of my fortune, both real " and perfonal, may be employ'd in erecting and " endowing a College for the holy order of Domi- " nican Friars; of which my pious and Right Re- " verend Chaplain Dominick Doubleface is to be " Superior, and in whofe hands this bequeft is to be " depofited, until the aforefaid College is com- " pleted." — And in whofe hands it is likely to re- main.—Poor credulous Don Pedro!—But pray, what is the difference between your intention and mine?— you leave your fortune to the church, and I convert it to the ufe of a churchman.

AIR THE FIFTH.

But when the rich treafure is mine,
No longer a Friar I'll be;
Away with the mafk of Divine,
When once it grows ufelefs to me.

[*Exit finging.*

The fcene changes to a green before a village, with a profpect of a grove on one fide; beyond which the top of a caftle appears.

EARL

EARL OF LEWINGTON *solus.*

It is almost nine weeks since I first took up my abode in this retired habitation, and, shelter'd beneath a rustic garb, have employ'd every moment in fruitless attempts of revealing myself to Clementina : but so strictly is she watch'd by that old female Argus, that I have never been able to obtain an interview, or even give her a hint of my disguise : and so cautious am I obliged to be, lest a discovery of my retreat should again expose me to the dangers I have lately escaped, that I am afraid to tamper with any of Don Pedro's domestics; who wou'd, in all probability, recollect my person, and betray me into the hands of my enemies.

AIR THE SIXTH.

Come, gentle Zephyr, lend thy aid,
Forsake yon gliding spring;
To seek the lovely weeping maid
Oh wave thy swiftest wing!

And when you find the blooming fair,
Oh tell her what I feel!
In plaintive murmurs to her ear,
My sighs, my vows reveal.

Enter

Enter SIR WILLIAM SANDBY.

SIR WILLIAM.

My dear Lewington! I'm heartily glad to fee you.

EARL OF LEWINGTON.

Ha! Sir William Sandby!—give me your hand. This generous proof of your friendfhip deferves my warmeft acknowledgments—it is a facrifice I was hardly felf-interefted enough to hope for.

SIR WILLIAM.

If it can deferve the name of a facrifice, it is one at leaft from which I derive the greateft advantage. But away with compliments, they are incompatible with fincerity, and tell me how have you amufed yourfelf in my abfence? Have you never once figh'd for the prohibited pleafures of a Court?

EARL OF LEWINGTON.

To prevent any fufpicion of my difguife, I appear as clownifh in my manners as my garb; affociate with my fellow-cottagers, and join freely in all their ruftic fports. Their converfation, indeed, is rude and unpolifh'd; but it is the language of the heart, and much lefs difgufting, to a rational ear, than the fmooth, ftudied eloquence of villains. And as for the Court, that neft of fools and bigots, every honeft man fhou'd fhun it—its very air is

infected

Infected with fuperftition; and nothing can furvive in fuch an atmofphere, but prieftcraft and hypocrify.

AIR the SEVENTH.

Wou'd Fortune my wealth and my honours return,
To depend on a Court, I her favours wou'd fpurn;
Reject the vain trifles, and boldly defpife
What villains obtain, and what fools only prize.

The man who ferene views the changes of Fate,
By frowns ne'er deprefs'd, nor by favours elate,
For int'reft or titles will never defcend
To barter his freedom, his faith, or his friend.

SIR WILLIAM.

To declare my fentiments with candour, Lew-ington, I am as heartily difgufted with the fuper-ftitious ignorance of our bigotted Court as you can poffibly be; I am therefore become a voluntary exile, determin'd to fhare the fortunes of my friend. But might we not pafs our time much more agree-ably in Holland, or a hundred other places, where we fhou'd be under no neceffity of appearing in dif-guife, than here among a parcel of peafants, whofe manners are as rude and uncultivated as their foil?

H 3 EARL

EARL OF LEWINGTON.

Oh, Sandby, I'm imprifon'd here!—A captive in the toils cf love.

SIR WILLIAM.

Ha, ha, ha! the philofophic Lewington at laft enflav'd by the charms of a woman!—Pray, who is the fair tyrant? Some gentle fhepherdefs or fylvan nymph, I fuppofe.

EARL OF LEWINGTON.

A lady of birth and fortune, equal to my moft afpiring wifhes. — Have you ever feen Clementina de Mendoza?

SIR WILLIAM.

What! the lovely daughter of Don Pedro de Mendoza, the Spanifh nobleman, who marry'd tho Earl of Darking's heirefs?

EARL OF LEWINGTON.

The fame.

SIR WILLIAM.

Your choice of a miftrefs affords me one more proof of your elegant tafte. But is this only a tranfient amour, or an attachment of a ferious nature?

EARL OF LEWINGTON.

So ferious, I affure you, that the future happinefs of my life depends upon it.——Clementina has

long

long honour'd me with her affections; and I had
once obtain'd her father's confent to our marriage:
but unfortunately, juſt at that crifis, my remon-
ftrances to Queen Mary, againſt the inhuman treat-
ment ſhewn towards the Princeſs Elizabeth, drew
upon me their Majefties difpleafure. I was declar'd a
traitor, and obliged to provide for my fafety by ab-
fconding; and immediately afterwards (on the de-
ceafe of Clementina's mother) Don Pedro (influ-
enced by an artful prieſt, who has an abfolute afcen-
dancy over him) determin'd to ſhew his zeal for
Popery, by condemning his daughter to a religious
life; and, to prevent any poffibility of her defeating
his intention, brought her down to yon ruinous
caftle, beyond the limits of whofe walls ſhe is not
permitted to ftray without an old maiden-fifter of
Don Pedro's, who is imagined to have too good an
underſtanding with the Friar, to let his intereſt fuffer by the efcape of her niece.

SIR WILLIAM.

Allow me to be your guide in the affair, and I'll
anfwer for it we releafe Clementina from her pri-
fon, tho' the Pope and all his myrmidons ſhou'd
guard her.

H 4   A I R

AIR the EIGHTH.

The gentle nymph whofe paffions move
Harmonious to the voice of love,
Difdains her freedom to refign,
Or in a gloomy convent pine.

Point out the path, fhe'll (fwiftly flying,
And harfh reftraint and bars defying)
Leave zealots to their vain alarms,
And feek protection in thy arms.

EARL OF LEWINGTON.

I know you are an adept in the fcience of intrigue, and from this moment acknowledge you my preceptor.

[*Grizilda paffes haftily over the further end of the ftage.*

SIR WILLIAM.

For Heaven's fake, Lewington, what fpecies of mortality moves yonder?

EARL OF LEWINGTON.

That's the dragon that guards the Hefperian fruit; Clementina's maiden-aunt.

SIR WILLIAM.

Enchant her, my friend, and bear away the prize.

EARL

EARL OF LEWINGTON.

Pſha!

SIR WILLIAM.

I am ſerious, upon my honour. Flattery is a powerful kind of muſic, which few women can re-ſiſt—it lulls the watchful ſenſes of enquiring jea-louſy, and ſmiles away ſuſpicion. Make love to the Duenna, and her Ward is your own.

EARL OF LEWINGTON.

Impoſſible !—'twould appear like inſulting her. Has ſhe not eyes to view her own deformity ?

SIR WILLIAM.

Flattery, flattery, Lewington, will make the ſex believe any thing. But I think ſhe ſeems to bend her ſteps this way; and, before ſhe comes too near, get you behind that tree, while I try what impreſ-ſion a few ſoft things will make on her heart.

AIR THE NINTH.

Tho' old and deform'd,
By flattery charm'd,
She'll fancy her graces renew;
And, vain of her power,
Believe you adore
The beauties which ne'er were her due.

With

With languishing eyes,
Soft accents and sighs,
You'll find free accefs to her heart:
Tho' frozen by age,
The paffions will rage
When Cupid has pointed a dart.

[*Lord Lewington goes behind a tree*
as Grizilda re-enters.

SIR WILLIAM.

Now flattery and impudence affift me !

GRIZILDA.

I'll warrant fhe's along with that faucy minx
Jenny ; but I'll be even with her—by our Lady, I
will.

SIR WILLIAM.

[*going up to Grizilda.*

You feem difcompos'd, Madam. May I prefume
to enquire the caufe of your perturbation ?

GRIZILDA.

Caufe ! why caufe enough to try the patience of
Saint Agnes, if fhe was in my fituation !

SIR WILLIAM.

Nay, calm yourfelf a little, I befeech you. Thofe
eyes were never form'd for anger, nor that brow for
frowns.

GRIZILDA.

For all your impertinent fneers, Sir, this fore-
head, and thofe eyes, have had their charms ; aye,
and their *admirers* too, I can affure you.

SIR WILLIAM.

You wrong me, Madam, by fufpecting my fincerity.—I can eafily imagine how formidable your
meridian beauty muft have been, fince even now I
feel the power of its declining luftre ;—but if your
fenfibility takes alarm at compliments, tho' ever fo
juftly due, I muft conceal the feelings of my heart,
and confine my expreffions to the cold limit of
efteem. But tho' I am forbid to fpeak my fentiments with freedom, I muft always admire in
filence thofe mental charms which time can never
impair.—Yes, Madam, 'tis that exalted virtue, which
even the tongue of envy dares not to traduce ; that
throws a thoufand namelefs graces round you,
and gives an air of dignity to your deportment,
which at once commands refpect and admiration.—
Might I prefume to hope your delicacy wou'd not
be wounded by my abruptnefs, I wou'd drop thofe
feeble epithets, and call the fentiments your merit
infpires by fofter names.

GRIZILDA.

Truly, Sir, this is a very extraordinary mode of
addrefs,

addrefs, and I do not know what conftruction to put on your behaviour.

SIR WILLIAM.

A lady of your penetration and good fenfe can never mifconftrue the language of refpect; and if my want of eloquence prevents my doing juftice to the fubject, I will rely on your candour to excufe the deficiency, and not fuffer it to injure me in your efteem.

GRIZILDA.

Injure you in my efteem!—really, Sir, I do not underftand what pretenfions you can have to my efteem.

SIR WILLIAM.

No pretenfions indeed, I muft confefs, but thofe which my profound refpect and admiration give me;—yet furely there is at leaft fome fmall degree of friendfhip due to one who has fo long and fo fincerely revered your virtues.

GRIZILDA.

Why, to be fure, there is fomething, as you fay, due to one who fhews us a preference;—but I really cannot recollect receiving any proof of yours, or indeed having ever feen you before in my life.

SIR WILLIAM.

I am concern'd to think, that a modeft diffidence fhou'd

fhou'd have thrown fuch a veil over the partiality I entertain for you, as to make me pafs entirely unnoticed.—It was the fear of offending, that always kept me at a diftance, and prevented my engaging your attention by any marks of mine.

G R I Z I L D A.

Pray, Sir, will you be fo kind as to inform me who you are, and where it was that I had the pleafure of being in your company!—Perhaps then I may be able to recollect fomething about you.

S I R   W I L L I A M.

The ftory of my life is fo diverfified with a variety of adventures, that it would require more leifure to unfold, than our prefent expos'd fituation will allow of—I have long fought an opportunity to divulge the interefting narrative to your ear ; and if you will honour me with attention at fome more convenient moment, my hiftory fhall be difclos'd without referve ; and cannot fail of rewarding your condefcenfion.

G R I Z I L D A.

I am afraid it will have the air of an affignation, if I confent to oblige you ; and yet, as you fay you have a fecret to communicate, I do not know how to refufe ;—fo you may come to the end of yonder

grove

grove at four o'clock this afternoon (perhaps I may take a walk that way)—and be sure you are very careful that nobody obferves you; for, as I am a fingle woman, my reputation might fuffer if I was to be feen alone with a man; and I wou'd not have my character impeach'd, no, not for her Majefty's dominions, and the wealth of Mexico to boot.

SIR WILLIAM.

You may rely on my fecrecy and caution. I know the value of a lady's reputation, and wou'd not injure your's for the univerfe.

GRIZILDA.

Then you may depend on my meeting you in the grove by four.

AIR THE TENTH.

There unfufpected I'll receive thee,
Since thou haft vow'd thou'lt not deceive me;
But fhou'd the prying world difcover,
They'd think I entertain'd a lover,
And I never cou'd my fame recover.
And I never cou'd, &c.   [*Exit* Grizilda.

[*Lord*

[Lord Lewington comes from behind the tree.

SIR WILLIAM.

Well, Lewington ! don't you think my intrigue wears a promifing afpect ?

EARL OF LEWINGTON.

Oh, Sandby, I am almoft difgufted with the fex !

SIR WILLIAM.

Wou'd my friend refufe to admire a beautiful picture, or a fine-proportion'd ftatue, becaufe he had feen a daub upon the fign-poft of an inn, or a diftorted Indian deity ?

EARL OF LEWINGTON.

Your reproof, my dear Sandby, does equal honour to your good fenfe and your generofity. But prithee how do you intend to fulfil your engagement with Grizilda ?—you won't meet her, furely ?

SIR WILLIAM.

Not I, faith.—I only made the appointment to fecure her for a while, and afford you an opportunity of revealing yourfelf to Clementina;—but if you find it neceffary to prolong her abfence from the caftle, I'll facrifice an hour to the intereft of my friend with all my heart.

EARL OF LEWINGTON.

How fhall I make a return to fuch generous and
disinterefted

ACT the SECOND.

[The former scene continues. The Earl of Lewington habited as a Pilgrim; Sir William Sandby as a Clown.]

SIR WILLIAM.

WHAT a powerful divinity is Love! who can instantaneously transform his votaries from courtiers into clowns—from cheerful shepherds to complaining pilgrims. Your disguise, my dear Lewington, is so exceedingly natural, that I was just going to enquire for what shrine you are destin'd.

EARL OF LEWINGTON.

For the shrine of an angel, my friend, where vows of love are to be the offering.—But do you think yourself sufficiently conceal'd by that habit to prevent your enamour'd Grizilda's detecting the imposition?

SIR WILLIAM.

Grizilda and I have not been many hours acquainted; and altering my voice a little will easily deceive her. Then, you know, the contents of this

letter

EARL OF LEWINGTON.

The great difparity between your rank and this amiable villager's, makes your mutual regard exceedingly unfortunate.

SIR WILLIAM.

The unaffected tendernefs fhe difcover'd for me, when I addrefs'd her under the difguife of a peafant, at our firft coming down, has made too deep an impreffion to be eafily obliterated; and though prudence and ambition both forbid our union, I am afraid it is impoffible that I fhould ever ceafe to love her. It was on her account alone that I wifh'd to remove from this agreeable retreat, left my growing paffion fhould at length obtain dominion over my honour, and in fome unguarded moment, when reafon lay abforb'd in tendernefs, perfuade me to forget the obligations which are due to love and unfufpecting innocence.

EARL OF LEWINGTON.

I am ftrangely interefted in the happinefs of that young creature, without being able to affign any reafon for the partiality I entertain in her favour; and yet I am not at all alarm'd for her on your account. Her native innocence, and the confidence fhe places in you, are fufficient guardians of her honour; for,

I   believe

believe me, Sandby, there is a majeſtic dignity in virtue, which awes the boldeſt libertine, and charms the
hawleſs paſſion of his heart to friendſhip and eſteem.

SIR WILLIAM.

I am entirely of your opinion, with reſpect to the
influence of female delicacy on a lover's conduct; but
ſtill, my friend, there are reaſons why I ought to ſhun
the means of increaſing a paſſion, which it may be
now in the power of time and abſence to eradicate.
I will avoid ſeeing her while I remain in the village,
and ſecure my retreat as ſoon as poſſible.

EARL OF LEWINGTON.

I commend your reſolution exceedingly, and wiſh
you may be able to perſevere.

AIR the TWELFTH.

But love, like ambition, unbounded, diſdains
That limit which paſſions leſs noble reſtrains ;
Like Neptune's proud waves, ſtill all laws will diſown,
And yield to the ſceptre of beauty alone.

SIR WILLIAM.

Yonder comes poor Grizilda, raging and foaming like the ſea in a ſtorm ;—let us retire before ſhe
8   obſerves

obferves us, and confult about the means of revealing you to Clementina.

[*Exeunt Lord Lewington and Sir William.*

Enter GRIZILDA *in a violent paffion, driving* JENNY *before her.*

GRIZILDA.

Out upon thee! out upon thee, naughty huffy!—but I'll rid the village of all fuch flirts: by our Lady, I will. Fine doings indeed! fine doings!—the world is come to a pretty pafs, when fuch impudent chits as you have the affurance to offer advice.

Enter ROGER.

ROGER.

Heyday!—Why, what's the matter now?

JENNY.

Only a hurricane, rais'd by envy and ill-nature—'twill foon blow over, Roger.

GRIZILDA.

Hold your prating, fauce-box!

ROGER.

Not fo foon, Jenny: It feems to threaten a tempeft.

GRIZILDA.

What's that you fay, fellow?—Oh, I have much ado to keep my temper, that I have! and only that I

I 2 wou'd

wou'd not make a hurry in the village, I'd carry ye both before Father Dominick this moment, and make him fend you to jail, and have ye tried for Heretics; that I would.

ROGER.

Hu—[*whistling*] you fpend your breath and your malice in vain, for I value you not. Come along, Jenny, and don't mind her. [*Taking Jenny's hand.*

GRIZILDA.

"Don't mind her!" truly—"don't mind her!" But you fhall rue your infolence, that you fhall, the moment my brother comes home.—"Don't mind her!"

DUET THE THIRTEENTH.

ROGER.

Nor you, nor your brother,
Nor forty fuch other,
Are worthy of Roger's regarding:
In honefty trufting,
A fig for your boafting:
I value you not of a farthing.

Your malice defpifing,
From envy arifing,
To fee the young Graces attend her:
Pray, guard your expreffion,
And bridle your paffion,
For while I have life I'll defend her.

GRIZILDA.

GRIZILDA.

You clown, you rude bear, you !
Oh how I cou'd tear you,
And claw that young minx for her fneering !
But that I may draw,
From the church and the law,
A vengeance more worthy your fearing.

JENNY.

Your anger fmoothe over,
Or elfe I'll difcover
An am'rous intrigue with a Friar.

ROGER, JENNY.

You'd better beware,
Or you'll tread on a fnare,
And entrap your own neck in the wire.

END OF THE FIRST ACT.

I 3   ACT

ACT the SECOND.

[The former scene continues. The Earl of Lewington habited as a Pilgrim; Sir William Sandby as a Clown.]

SIR WILLIAM.

WHAT a powerful divinity is Love! who can instantaneously transform his votaries from courtiers into clowns—from cheerful shepherds to complaining pilgrims. Your disguise, my dear Lewington, is so exceedingly natural, that I was just going to enquire for what shrine you are destin'd.

EARL OF LEWINGTON.

For the shrine of an angel, my friend, where vows of love are to be the offering.—But do you think yourself sufficiently conceal'd by that habit to prevent your enamour'd Grizilda's detecting the imposition?

SIR WILLIAM.

Grizilda and I have not been many hours acquainted; and altering my voice a little will easily deceive her. Then, you know, the contents of this

letter

letter will make her believe me fifty miles diftant at leaft, and confequently remove all fufpicion.

EARL OF LEWINGTON.

Surely, Sandby, Cupid himfelf is your infpiring genius, or you cou'd never be fuch a proficient in the fcience of gallantry!—But I fuppofe, by this time, the old lady is approaching the place of affignation, to meet you, and in the interim I'll repair to the Caftle.

DUET THE FOURTEENTH.

Oh Cupid! no longer, my paffion defpifing,
Condemn me to languifh, a prey to defpair!
Oh pity the fmart from thy arrow arifing,
And kindly refign the dear nymph to my pray'r!

SIR WILLIAM.

With foothing perfuafion fhe'll yield to thy
    paffion;
Her bofom relenting, will foften to love:
Away then, go pay your devotion;
With fmiles the fair faint will your duty approve.

[*Exeunt feverally.*

I 4   *Enter*

Enter ROGER.

AIR THE FIFTEENTH.

As Jenny turns the new-mown hay,
She looks as fweet, as blithe as May,
And rofy as the rifing day,
Afcending o'er yon mountain :
When fhe her pails at evening brings,
To milk the kine, and fweetly fings,
Her voice is foft as murm'ring fprings,
Which glide from yonder fountain.

But when on holyday fhe's feen
In fprightly dance to trip the green,
Her fhape, her face, her graceful mien,
Make ev'ry fwain her lover.

[*Enter* JENNY.

Oh Jenny! wou'dft thou be but mine,
My flocks, my herds, my brindled kine,
What I poffefs fhall all be thine,
And I'll be true for ever.

JENNY.

I wifh, Roger, you wou'd find fome other fubject
to entertain me with ; this is grown fo tirefome, I
am quite difgufted with it.

AIR

AIR THE SIXTEENTH.
Oh, Roger, ceafe to teaze me,
I never can be thine;
Willy alone can pleafe me;
For him, alas! I pine.

My heart he ftill poffeffes,
Since in the beechen grove,
With many fond careffes,
He vow'd eternal love.   [*Exeunt.*

[The fcene changes to an avenue, with a caftle at the
extreme end; Clementina and Grizilda coming
towards the gates. The Earl of Lewington, in his
pilgrim's habit, enters about the middle of the
avenue, and is going towards the caftle; but on
feeing Clementina, ftops fhort, leans a while upon
his ftaff, and then feats himfelf on the root of a
tree.]

AIR THE SEVENTEENTH.
CLEMENTINA.
Some friendly pow'r her anger foothe!
Incline her to attend!
        [*Turning to Grizilda.*]
Can the gay fmiles of fprightly youth,
Can innocence offend?

                                    Oh

Oh let my humble forrow move:
An ear of pity lend:
Hear my complaint, my fuit approve;
Reftore my gentle friend!

GRIZILDA.   [angrily.

I tell you, Clementina, you may as well leave off
your whining; for I have given pofitive directions,
that Jenny fhou'd not be fuffer'd within thefe walls;
—and if fhe gets in by ftratagem, and I catch you together, you fhall both have reafon to repent it all
your lives, I promife you.

CLEMENTINA.

How cruel it is to deprive me of the only blefling
I enjoy'd, by forbidding me the converfation of that
dear innocent girl!—Was it not enough to condemn
me to a convent, that you muft embitter my few re-
maining hours of liberty, by prohibiting the only indulgence that made life agreeable!

GRIZILDA.

You'd better not provoke me, Clementina: you'd
better not provoke me—for depend upon it, I'll be
even with you; that I will.—Here, take this book,
[giving one] and go back to your chamber, and ftudy
it till my return, for I am going to attend four o'clock
vefpers at Saint Catherine's; and as I intend to fit a
little

little with the Abbefs, perhaps I may not be at home for an hour or two; but on your peril be it, if you difobey my commands.   [*Exit.*

[Clementina fits down on a bank, while the Earl of Lewington rifes and comes forward unperceived by her.]

CLEMENTINA.

Sure, my unhappy life is ordain'd for one continued fcene of mifery!

AIR THE EIGHTEENTH.

Farewell, fweet illufions! gay fhadows, adieu!
In fancy no more I'll vain pleafures purfue:
   Deluded by them, I rove,
   Wild as the thoughts of love,
Vainly revolving the fcenes I'd renew.

Ye Breezes, ye Zephyrs, who fan the cool air,
And thou, gentle Echo, oh hither repair;
   And breathing plaintive fighs
   On ev'ry gale that flies,
Teach all thy haunts to refound my defpair!

CLEMENTINA.

Lewington! oh Lewington, where doft thou roam?—Exil'd, profcrib'd; perhaps ere now betray'd!

tray'd!—Juft Heaven avert the thought, and fhield
him from the rage of lawlefs tyranny! Guard him,
ye Angels, guard my Lewington; and in return for
all the miferies which I endure, crown him with
bleffings!

[The Earl comes up to her, fupported on his ftaff,
and difguifes his voice as he fpeaks.]

EARL OF LEWINGTON.

Alas! fweet lady, why are you thus afflicted?
Sure, forrow is a bold intruder, to ufurp dominion
o'er your gentle heart!—Excufe an old man's freedom; but methinks, that melancholy look betrays a
love-fick mind.

CLEMENTINA.

[Afide.] He has furely overheard me; and on that
account, believing himfelf acquainted with a fecret,
grows infolent. —[To him.] You're much miftaken,
friend, in your furmife: perhaps I mourn the lofs of
a relation, or fome other unfortunate event.

EARL OF LEWINGTON.

My fenfes, fure, deceived me, or I heard my Clementina mourn the abfence of her Lewington.
    [Throwing back his hood, and difcovering himfelf.

CLEMENTINA.

CLEMENTINA.

Heavens!

EARL OF LEWINGTON.

[*Receiving her in his arms.*

Oh Clementina! my kind, my generous Clementina! pronounce thofe foft, thofe foothing founds
again :—fay that you love ; there's magic in the
found; 'twill charm away my cares, and make me
bleft, in fpite of wayward fortune.

CLEMENTINA.

My heart beats in unifon with your's, and melts
with fympathizing tendernefs ; yet I muft filence its
foft notes, and play the monitor.—Think of the dangers that furround us, and of the confequences which
muft enfue if we are feen together!

EARL OF LEWINGTON.

Love, and the filent voice of Nature, bid us fly
thofe dangers while the prefent moment favours our
efcape. A proper difguife is already provided, and
every thing neceffary for your reception.

CLEMENTINA.

Alas! my Lord, a father's abfolute commands op-
pofe it.

EARL OF LEWINGTON.

Will my Clementina then obey that cruel father,
and

and devote this beauteous form to the harsh austeri-
ties of a monastic life ?—Forbid it, Heaven !

AIR THE NINETEENTH.

Like blighted rose-buds, doom'd to fade
In some dark convent's lonely shade,
Let nymphs adorn'd with fainter charms
Fly from the reach of fond alarms.

While we the fleeting hours improve,
Obedient to the voice of Love ;
Nor idly drop a useless tear,
But share a sweet elysium here.

CLEMENTINA.

Ah ! wherefore are love and obedience incompatible—or why is my irresolute heart incapable of
relinquishing either attachment ?

EARL OF LEWINGTON.

Let me decide the conflict, and conduct you to a
place of safety !   [*He endeavours to lead her off.*

CLEMENTINA.

                    [*Drawing back her hand.*
Forbear to urge me, my Lord ;—I must not go;—
indeed I must not.

                                        EARL

EARL OF LEWINGTON.

Perhaps my Clementina scorns to share a ship-wreck'd fortune;—if so, farewell for ever.

AIR THE TWENTIETH.

That form where youth and beauty reign,
Where dwell ten thousand graces,
Will never bind a lover's chain,
If pride each charm debases.

CLEMENTINA.

Unkind Lewington! how can you indulge such cruel suspicions!—Have I not already given you a thousand proofs of my regard; and, if you require one of my confidence, I solemnly assure you that I will fly to your arms for protection, if I cannot avoid the veil by any milder means.

EARL OF LEWINGTON.

Thou gentle excellence! why, why did I suspect thee?—Oh Clementina, excess of tenderness gave rise to my resentment. I could not bear the idea of your regard's being less generous and disinterested than my own.

DUET

DUET the TWENTY-FIRST.

Was Britain's regal sceptre mine,
Her fame, her wealth's unbounded measure,
For thee those blessings I'd resign;
Thy smile's my crown, my joy, my treasure.

CLEMENTINA.

Tho' danger mark'd the dreary way,
From softer scenes of pleasure flying,
Thro' desert wilds with thee I'd stray,
The angry frown of Fate defying.

BOTH.

Tyrant Duty! yield thy sway;
Now gentle Love assumes his throne;
The God inspires, and we obey,
Resign'd to his commands alone.   *Exeunt.*

[The scene changes to the end of a grove.]

GRIZILDA *alone.*

Was ever a woman so insulted, so abused?—Here
have I been almost a full hour, waiting for a fellow
who, I suppose, never intended to meet me.—A
pretty

pretty piece of bufinefs, truly ! a pretty piece of bufinefs I have made of it !

[*As fhe is going off in a violent paffion, Sir William,
in the habit of a clown, meets her.*]

SIR WILLIAM.

Pray, ben't your name dame Grizil ?

GRIZILDA.

Fellow, my name is Donna Grizilda.

SIR WILLIAM.

Isn't this letter for you ?

[*She takes the letter from him impatiently, opens and
reads it.*]

GRIZILDA.

Oh the dear obliging creature !—Indeed, I cou'd
hardly think he intended to deceive me. [*She
reads.*] " Yes, Madam, I will fly on the wings of
" impatience to the end of the Grove, by fix o'clock
" to-morrow evening, and explain the reafon of my
" feeming negleƈt, in fuch a manner as muft enfure
" my pardon, and make you pity rather than con-
" demn me." [*To Sir William.*] And pray, where
have you been loitering all this while, you great
lout you ? I fhou'd have had this letter near an
hour ago.

K

SIR WILLIAM.

Your Honour——I only ſtaid to ſee old Goody
Teſty duck'd in 'Squire Quorum's horſe-pond for a
witch.

GRIZILDA.

Get out of my ſight, blockhead, and don't provoke
me!

SIR WILLIAM.

[*Scratching his head.*

I hope your Ladyſhip will conſider a poor lad, who
came out of his way to oblige you.

GRIZILDA.

There, [*in taking out money to give him, ſhe drops a
paper from her pocket.*] take that, and get about your
buſineſs.

[*Sir William retires into the grove, and Grizilda
comes forward.*]

AIR the TWENTY-SECOND.

Oh, if the youth ſhou'd worthy prove,
I'll, Dominick, diſcard thee;
And while I'm happy in his love,
E'en let the Church feward thee.

For

For thou may'ft pine,
My niece too whine,
And burft with mere vexation;
But when a bride,
I'll both deride
With fcorn and indignation. [*Exit*.

[*Sir William comes forward from among the trees.*]

SIR WILLIAM.

Oh woman, woman! what a medley art thou of
ftorms and fun-fhine! This moment more out-
rageous than the northern blaft, and the next footh'd
to an halcyon calm by the delufive voice of flattery!
[*Seeing the paper Grizilda had dropt, he takes it up.*]
Ha! what have I here? A paper moft curioufly
folded: perhaps, it contains my enamorato's laft-
drawn Valentine. Now, curiofity, to obey thy dictates. [*He opens it.*] Ha, ha, ha! one of the Friar's
love-letters! [*He reads.*] " Dominick Doubleface
" to his dear and loving fifter Grizilda de Mendoza."
[*He looks at the bottom.*] No faith, this is fomething of a more ferious nature; for here's a broad
feal at the bottom.——What the devil! a Deed!
whereby he acknowledges an obligation to marry
her, as foon as he becomes poffefs'd of her brother
Don Pedro's fortune!—— Prithee, Lucifer, refign
the palm of hypocrify! for I think thou art rivall'd

K 2 at

at laſt.——Now let me ſee what this indenture further witneſſeth : [*he reads.*] " That if I the ſaid Do-
" minick ſhould refuſe to marry thee the ſaid Gri-
" zilda, thou ſhalt, on ſuch refuſal, be entitled to the
" one half of whatever fortune I ſhall then enjoy."
——This may be of infinite advantage to my friend
Lewington, in his affair with Clementina ; for, in
all probability, the old Jezabel will conſent to favour her niece's eſcape, if by that means ſhe can
ſuppreſs this ſcene of villainy.

AIR the TWENTY-THIRD.

She who religion and virtue abuſes,
(Deep in hypocriſy hiding
Vices indulg'd) while the world ſhe amuſes,
By female frailties chiding ;
Rather than loſe
The means to impoſe,
Will freely make any conceſſions you chuſe.

[*Exit.*

[The ſcene changes to the Green before the village.]

ROGER *ſolus.*

It is all in vain ! for I can think of nothing but
Jenny. Her indifference diſtracts me, and I wander
about

about my farm like a forlorn traveller in a wilder-
nefs.—I will e'en difpofe of my effects, and try my
fortune at fea ; for the 'oftener I behold her the
more unhappy I grow.

AIR THE TWENTY-FOURTH.

> Since Jenny flights my paffion,
> Ye native plains, adieu!
> I'll feek the ftormy ocean,
> Lefs favage now than you.

> The foaming waves afcending,
> The dangers of the main,
> Nor all the winds contending,
> Can equal her difdain.

Enter SIR WILLIAM, *in the drefs of a Peafant.*

SIR WILLIAM.

Ha! my old friend Roger! give me your hand.
—You look dejected.—What's the matter?

ROGER.

Methinks, Mafter William, I can't help wifhing
I had never feen you.

SIR WILLIAM.

Why fo, Roger? What have I done to offend
you?

K 3   ROGER.

ROGER.

Before you came to our village, I think I ftood as well with Jenny as another did ; and tho', I believe, fhe did not love me, it was fome fatisfaction to know fhe lov'd nobody elfe. But I know not how it is, your fine ftories have fet her quite befide her-felf — fhe can think of nothing, nor talk of no-thing, but you.

SIR WILLIAM.

If that's all, Roger, we fhall foon be friends again.—I'll teach you the way to win her, my ho-neft fellow.

AIR THE TWENTY-FIFTH.

Oh Roger, wou'dft thou win a lafs,
Diffemble, flatter, praife her,
Until fhe thinks her looking-glafs
Of half her charms betrays her.

Swear that her eyes as ftars are bright,
Her cheeks like new-blown rofes,
And that the lily's fnowy white
Her lovely neck difclofes.

Swear

Swear that she breathes the sweets of spring;
That wanton Cupids hover
Around her form on airy wing,
To wound the trembling lover.

Thus, Roger, wou'dst thou win a lass,
Dissemble, flatter, praise her;
Her charms she'll think thou can't surpass,
While vanity betrays her.

ROGER.

Ah that I had but such a tongue as yours! However, I'll try what I can do; and if I succeed, you shall come to the wedding, I promise you. [*Exit.*

Manet SIR WILLIAM.

Poor Roger! I pity thee from my soul! but thy honest simplicity in discovering Jenny's tender remembrance of me, has renew'd my affection, and will make me break through every resolution I had form'd of avoiding her.——Oh Fortune, Fortune! why didst thou place so great a difference between our birth? Wou'd that my soul inspir'd the form of some contented villager! or that my Jenny cou'd be rais'd to the exalted sphere her merit wou'd so eminently grace!——Yonder she comes! smiling like the morn, and adorn'd with all the charms

of

of youth and innocence!—[*Enter Jenny, with a bunch of flowers in her hand.*]—Ha! Jenny! where are you tripping in such haste? I was juft going to your mother's, to enquire for you.

JENNY.

Pray, Willy, how long have you been arrived? I began to think you never intended to vifit our village again.

SIR WILLIAM.

Did my little angel regret my abfence?

JENNY.

I don't know.

SIR WILLIAM.

Whofe hedges have you been robbing of thefe honeyfuckles?

JENNY.

Only our old walk by the grove-fide.

SIR WILLIAM.

Did not that fcene awake a train of tender ideas, and fwell thy gentle bofom with a figh for my return?—'Twas there I often pluck'd the new-blown violet for you; and, when a fudden fhow'r obliged us to take fhelter in a thicket, amufed your ear with tales of love, and vows of everlafting conftancy.

JENNY.

JENNY.

Wou'd I had never liften'd to them!

SIR WILLIAM.

Why fo?

JENNY.

My mother fays, they were only intended to deceive me.

SIR WILLIAM.

And can you believe her, Jenny?

DUET THE TWENTY-SIXTH.

SIR WILLIAM.

The lawlefs libertine may rove
Thro' love's deftructive wiles;
By Honour's rules my paffions move,
Tho' fann'd by Beauty's fmiles.

JENNY.

Secure in native innocence,
My heart no fears fhall own;
Away, Diftruft! Sufpicion, hence!
Each idle doubt is flown.

BOTH.

BOTH.

To scenes where pride and av'rice reign,
Let Jealousy repair,
There haunt the gay fantastic train,
But shun the artless fair.   [*Exeunt.*

[*Enter the Earl of Lewington in his pilgrim's habit, Sir William seeing him, returns.*]

SIR WILLIAM.

A very respectable figure indeed !——But a truce
with Ave-maries, and tell me how has that garb of
sanctity succeeded ?

EARL OF LEWINGTON.

So much to my satisfaction, that I intend reserv-
ing it for such another occasion. [*Taking off his pilgrim's gown.*] At six o'clock to-morrow evening
this said sable habit is to introduce me again to Clementina.

SIR WILLIAM.

Then she has consented to go off with you ?

EARL OF LEWINGTON.

Not quite :—but she has promis'd to fly to me for
protection, rather than take the veil.

SIR WILLIAM.

After such a concession, you may easily persuade
her to elope ; for when once a woman listens to the
allur-

alluring voice of temptation, fhe is half inclined to yield to the tempter.

EARL OF LEWINGTON.

Did you learn that maxim from any condefcenfion of Jenny's, before you parted juft now?

SIR WILLIAM.

I thought your inquifitive eyes wou'd difcover her.

EARL OF LEWINGTON.

Ha! Sandby, Sandby! where is all your boafted refolution?

SIR WILLIAM.

Difperfed like a vapour by the fun-beams.—But to be ferious for a moment, Lewington: There is fomething in that lovely girl which almoft convinces me fhe is not of vulgar extraction. She wears indeed the habit of rufticity, but at the fame time fhe difcovers a noblenefs and generofity of foul which diftinguifh her from the village-race.

EARL OF LEWINGTON.

How willingly we adopt an opinion, tho' ever fo abfurd, if it feems to flatter our affections!

SIR WILLIAM.

I acknowledge the juftnefs of your obfervation;—but let her birth be ever fo obfcure, fhe is render'd more illuftrious by her virtues than all the empty
titles

titles in the univerſe cou'd make her. At leaſt, ſhe ſeems ſufficiently ennobled by them, in my opinion, to offer her my hand.

EARL OF LEWINGTON.

What will the world ſay, when they behold the gay Sir William Sandby (who rov'd with careleſs indifference thro' the circle of an accompliſh'd Court) neglect thoſe beauties who are univerſally admired, and chuſe for life a ſimple villager?

SIR WILLIAM.

They'll cenſure tho' they envy my felicity;—but while my own heart and that of my friend approve my conduct, I can laugh at the ſarcaſms of malice and ill-nature.

EARL OF LEWINGTON.

Excuſe me, Sandby, if I ſtarted that objection as a trial of your fortitude. I know your ſoul is noble, generous, and diſintereſted; but I was willing to put your reſolution to the teſt.—There are too few who can ſtand the ſhock of ridicule, tho' in ever ſo worthy a cauſe; and that man muſt poſſeſs an unuſual ſhare of heroiſm who dares to brave it.

DUET

DUET the TWENTY-SEVENTH.

SIR WILLIAM.

No tyrant cuftom awes
Where Love maintains his fway;
He reigns by nobler laws,
And willing hearts obey.

EARL OF LEWINGTON.

Sweet magic of a fmile
Can charm Ambition down,
And one fond look beguile
Stern Pride's oppofing frown.

BOTH.

'Tis Love's peculiar pow'r
To harmonize the foul;
To calm the ftorms that lowr,
And jarring thoughts controul.

Sweet peace furrounds his throne,
While pleafures wait his nod;
Nor cares nor fears are known
To thofe who own the God.   [*Exeunt.*

END OF THE SECOND ACT.

9   ACT

ACT THE THIRD.

Scene a hall in the caftle.

Enter FATHER DOMINICK *and* GRIZILDA.

GRIZILDA.

BY our Lady, one had need have the eyes of an Argus, to be a match for fuch an intriguing baggage :—but I'll be even with her;—I'll teach her to make appointments—by our Lady, I will. A fine piece of work, truly, if fhe had made her efcape!

FATHER DOMINICK.

Your indignation againft Clementina makes you overlook one of the principal advantages arifing from this difcovery.—You have forgot the great reward offered by our pious Queen for apprehending that traitor Lewington.

GRIZILDA.

Oh, Father Dominick! what fpecial care Heaven takes to bring all thefe vile heretics to juftice!—But are you certain they did not difcover you?

FATHER DOMINICK.

Yes, very certain; for, as I was telling you, there

6

was

was fuch convenient fhelter, that I crept almoft clofe to them, and lay fnug, until they left the avenue, and went down the Yew Walk; and then, crawling on all fours on the other fide of the hedge, I heard them plan the whole affair :—how, if fhe was at all alarm'd, and had not time to give him intelligence of it, fhe was to repair in difguife to his cottage at the end of the village, and they were to efcape together to Holland.

GRIZILDA.

Lord have mercy upon us! what artifices there are in this wicked world!

Enter CLEMENTINA.

CLEMENTINA.

Pray, Madam, what did you want me for in fuch a violent hurry?

GRIZILDA.

To prevent your difhonouring your family, you gracelefs baggage, you!—to prevent your eloping with that traitor, Lewington!

CLEMENTINA.

What can this mean?

GRIZILDA.

You won't have the affurance to deny it, I hope, when here's Father Dominick overheard the whole
plot

plot concerted.—Oh ! I have much ado to keep my hands off you !—my fingers itch to pull down that proud fpirit of yours.—Aye, I knew your father wou'd bring nothing but difgrace upon his head by marrying your heretic mother. I told him what he might expect from it—but he wou'd not regard my admonitions.

FATHER DOMINICK.

Hark thee, Grizilda; a word in thy ear :—I want to advife with thee about fecuring the Earl.

[*They talk apart, while Clementina comes forward.*

CLEMENTINA.

This is indeed too much !——I cou'd have borne my own misfortunes, tho' they were fevere ; but when I reflect on Lewington's danger, my refolution fails, and I am almoft diftracted !

AIR the TWENTY-EIGHTH.

If tears can perfuade, or if forrow can move,
Attend, gentle Venus, bright Goddefs of Love!
Relieve my affliction, my anguifh relieve,
And lend thy affiftance their fchemes to deceive!

But

, But if unregarded I vainly implore,
Or figh for loft pleafures thou canft not reftore;
Yet hear me, fair Queen, to thy vot'ry attend,
And Lewington ftill from all danger defend !

GRIZILDA.

Aye, aye, Father Dominick, you may depend on
my caution.—I'll take care of Madam, while you
raife a party to feize her gallant :—for, as you juftly
obferve, if you was to attack him without affiftance,
he might prove too many for you ; and being a heretic, he wou'd fhew no refpect to your facred
perfon.

FATHER DOMINICK.

But be fure, Grizilda, that you do not fuffer her
to give him the leaft intimation of my defign.

GRIZILDA.

Never fear, never fear.—I think, I am not fo eafily
over-reach'd as that comes to; neither.—[*To Clementina.*] In with you to your chamber this moment,
Miftrefs ; in with you, I fay—and take my word
for it you come out no more till your father returns ;
and then fee if he will releafe you, when he hears of
your pretty goings-on.

L   CLEMENTINA.

CLEMENTINA.

Tho' my father left me under your care, he did not give you authority to imprifon me :—and I won't fubmit to confinement.

GRIZILDA.

Is not her infolence enough to provoke a Saint, Father Dominick?

AIR THE TWENTY-NINTH.

Was ever fuch a faucy jade!
(By neither fhame or duty fway'd)
Who dar'd a parent's pow'r invade!
Get in, for I will be obey'd.

[*Exit Grizilda, driving Clementina before her.*

FATHER DOMINICK *folus.*

What a lucky fellow am I! This clinches the whole affair.—Don Pedro loves his daughter; and tho' he yielded to my perfuafions, yet he betray'd great concern at forcing her into a convent againft her confent; but this difcovery clinches it.—He can never think of leaving her at liberty, after having an intrigue with an heretic.——So I have nothing to do now but fecure Lewington, and then I think my fortune is made.

AIR

AIR the THIRTIETH.

Shou'd the bufy tongue of Envy
Brand me with a villain's name,
I'll reply—Tho' you condemn me,
For my prize you'd act the fame.

[*Exit finging.*]

Enter GRIZILDA.

Aye, aye, " Safe bind, fafe find," as the proverb
fays.—Here is the key of Clementina's chamber in
my pocket; and unlefs fhe can procure a pair of
wings, and fly out of the window, I think fhe is in
no likelihood of efcaping from my clutches.—So far
things are as they fhould be :—and now let me con-
fider about fome feafible means of breaking with
Dominick, if I find my young lover better worth
my acceptance. —By our Lady, I think I out-
witted the Friar, when I prevail'd on him to fign
that Agreement ; for now I am fure of half my brother's fortune, at any rate : aye, and half his own
into the bargain.

Enter a Servant.

SERVANT.

Madam, Don Pedro is juft arrived.

GRIZILDA.

GRIZILDA.

What! my brother come home! Why, I did not expect him this fortnight.—Well, I'll e'en go and have the first story, before he fees Clementina, or perhaps, by telling a Canterbury tale, she may persuade him to forgive her; for he is such a foolish old dotard, that he hardly knows how to refuse her any thing.   [*Exeunt.*

[Scene changes to the Green before the village]

Enter SIR WILLIAM SANDBY *and* JENNY.

JENNY.

Believe me, Willy, you mistake the motive of my behaviour:—for, painful as this instance of obedience is, a mother's absolute command enjoins it, and obliges me to bid you an everlasting adieu.

SIR WILLIAM.

Too lovely, but too insensible girl!——is it possible, that, deaf to all my sighs, my vows, and my intreaties, you can still resolve to dedicate your youth and beauty to the whimsical perverseness of age, and indulge a mother's caprice rather than a lover's prayer?

JENNY.

JENNY.

If you regard my happiness, forbear to importune me.

AIR THE THIRTY-FIRST.

Cease, too lovely youth, to charm me!
Cease, nor by those sighs disarm me!
Duty's cruel laws must sway me,
Nor relenting love betray me.

SIR WILLIAM.

Oh thou obdurate creature!

DUET THE THIRTY-SECOND.

SIR WILLIAM.

See how I languish!
Pity my anguish!
Save a fond youth who depends on thy smile!
Vainly admiring,
Trembling, expiring,
Snatch me from death, and my sorrows beguile!

L 3   JENNY.

JENNY.

Eyes fondly pleading,
Love interceding,
Soften my heart and its torments renew,
Cruel intrusion !
Fly, fond delusion !
Duty and prudence command this adieu,

[*Exit* JENNY,

SIR WILLIAM.

[*looking after* JENNY.

Oh Jenny ! do I love, and yet allow that dear
gentle bosom to be torn with such a tumult of con-
tending passions, when it is in my power to calm
them ? — No; I will follow thee, and make a full
confession of my rank, and of my honourable intentions :—these will surely dispel a mother's fears, and
remove every obstacle that impedes our union.

[*Exit.*

Enter FATHER DOMINICK.

Heyday ! What can be the meaning of all this ?
—Is it the effect of caprice or temerity ?——Strict
injunctions from Don Pedro to dismiss my attend-
ants, without attempting to seize Lewington, and
repair to the castle immediately !—A vexatious disap-
pointment, by Saint Dominick !—Thousand pound
premiums

premiums are not to be pick'd up every day.——
However, the old Don muſt be humour'd in ſome
points, if I mean to ſucceed in others. So fare thee
well, Lewington, for the preſent ; but depend on
the word of a Friar, I'll never loſe ſcent of thee,
until I have at leaſt had ſnacks in the reward for apprehending thee.   [*Exit.*

Enter the EARL OF LEWINGTON *and*
        CLEMENTINA.

CLEMENTINA.

Availing myſelf of the general confuſion occaſioned by my father's unexpected return, I found
means to get off, with the aſſiſtance of an old faithful ſervant, whoſe ſecrecy I can depend on : and let
me conjure you, my Lord, to fly from the impend-
ing danger — the approaching night will favour
your eſcape.

EARL OF LEWINGTON.

No, Clementina; ſince you refuſe to be the part-
ner of my flight, why ſhould I endeavour to prolong a wretched exiſtence, which wou'd only be a
curſe without thee?

CLEMENTINA.

Oh, Lewington! if your love was as ſincere as
mine, you wou'd not thus reſolve to ſacrifice a life

so neceffary to my happinefs.—Tho' a too rigorous
fate forbids me to accompany you at prefent, we yet
may meet under the influence of a milder deftiny.—
Let that idea prevail on you to feek fecurity, for my
fake, if not for your own.—[*Sir, William enters at
the further end of the ftage.*]—Good God! we are
difcover'd!—Fly, fly, my Lord, and remember of
what confequence your life is to Clementina!

[*Exit Clementina.*

[*Sir William runs to Lord Lewington, and
embraces him.*]

SIR WILLIAM.

Oh, my friend, I wou'd congratulate you!—I
wou'd tell you how fincerely I participate your approaching felicity:—but all language is too dull to
exprefs the feelings of my heart!

EARL OF LEWINGTON.

Ha! Sandby! you are much miftaken. Thefe
congratulations are but ill-timed—Behold in me
the moft unhappy wretch that Nature ever form'd!

SIR WILLIAM.

Forget thefe melancholy thoughts, and look forward to a brighter fcene that dawns upon you.

EARL OF LEWINGTON.

You fport with my misfortunes, Sandby! Is
that acting like a friend?

SIR WILLIAM.

. Your too juft refentment has awaken'd me.—I
own I was to blame for holding you one moment ·
in fufpence on an affair of fuch confequence as the
event which gives rife to my tranfports.—Queen
Mary is dead, and the Princefs Elizabeth fecurely
feated on the Britifh throne!——It was this extraordinary change of government that occafioned Don
Pedro's fudden return ; and it has alfo procured us
a vifit from our old friend Lord Clayton, who is this
moment arrived with difpatches from the young
Queen, requiring your immediate attendance at
Court, to receive thofe honours and rewards which
are due to your long and faithful fervices.

EARL OF LEWINGTON.

Juft Heavens! what a reverfe of fortune!

SIR WILLIAM.

May every one that chequers the life of my friend
be equally agreeable!

EARL OF LEWINGTON.

I thank you, my dear Sandby, moft fincerely;
—but

—but while Clementina's liberty is in danger, almost all events are alike indifferent to me!

SIR WILLIAM.

Will you permit me to try what I can do with her father?—You know I am acquainted with some secrets which may probably have great influence with him.

EARL OF LEWINGTON.

With all my heart,—Go, and success attend you!

SIR WILLIAM.

Adieu!—May Fortune be my friend on this, as on former occasions!   [Exit.

Manet LORD LEWINGTON.

Queen Mary dead! and Elizabeth upon the throne!—I can't believe my senses!—and yet I have no room to doubt it.—'Twas Sandby told the news, and he is incapable of deceiving me.

Enter MRS. WILSON, *leading in* JENNY.

MRS. WILSON.

Pardon this intrusion, Sir, and give me leave to enquire if you are not the Earl of Lewington?

EARL OF LEWINGTON.

I am, Madam.—Pray what are your commands?

M R.1.

MRS. WILSON.

Obferve the features of this young creature, my
Lord! [*prefenting Jenny.*] She is now juft eighteen!

EARL OF LEWINGTON.

I had a fifter once, who, if alive, wou'd be about
that age; but fhe was fhipwreck'd with my mother, when fhe fled to avoid the dangers that threaten'd her, after the unfortunate fall of her coufin
Ann Bullen.

MRS. WILSON.

'Twas I invented that ftory to deceive the world!
—In Jenny behold that fifter!—and as an evidence
of her birth, fhe is mark'd on the left arm with a
rofe-bud;—which your Lordfhip muft certainly
remember.

EARL OF LEWINGTON.

I do indeed!—Heavens! is it poffible!—My
fifter! [*Embracing her.*

JENNY.

Oh my brother! [*Falling on his bofom.*

EARL OF LEWINGTON.

Tell me in a moment, thou excellent woman!
by what miracle was fhe preferv'd?

MRS. WILSON.

Before the Countefs, your mother, embark'd for

Holland, fhe committed that lady to my care, with ftrict injunctions to conceal her quality, and treat her as my own child.—On the melancholy news of the Countefs being caft away, I remov'd to this fequefter'd village; and changing my name from Levenage to Wilfon, I pretended that fhe was my daughter—as fuch indeed I love her—but, as far as my abilities extended, I have accomplifh'd her according to her birth; and tho' fhe has been educated in a cottage, fhe'll not difgrace a Court.——— The late happy revolution of government induced me to make immediate enquiry about your Lordfhip, and I have been fortunate enough to fucceed beyond my hopes.

EARL OF LEWINGTON.

Thou worthy! thou ineftimable woman! how fhall I exprefs my gratitude for this uncommon inftance of fidelity! or the joy I feel at the recovery of a long-lamented fifter!

MRS. WILSON.

. The pleafure of feeing her reftor'd to a brother's protection, makes me ample amends for the duty I have perform'd.

10   *Enter*

Enter SIR WILLIAM SANDBY.

EARL OF LEWINGTON.

Approach, my friend! and receive from her brother's hand the juft reward of your generous and
difinterefted love. [*Prefenting Jenny.*

SIR WILLIAM.

A brother's hand!—what can this mean?

EARL OF LEWINGTON.

She is indeed my fifter, my dear, my only fifter.
—At another opportunity I will inform you of the
circumftances of her prefervation; but the moments
are now too precious, and I am impatient to learn
your fuccefs with Don Pedro.

SIR WILLIAM.

Is Jenny then the fifter of Lewington? [*Embracing her.*] There wanted only this to complete
my felicity.—But I muft not fuffer my own happinefs to prevent my attending to that of my friend.
—I have prepared Don Pedro for a full difcovery of
the plot between the Friar and Grizilda, and muft
leave it to you to produce their Agreement whenever
you think it will be moft conducive to your intereft.
—He waits for your Lordfhip in the avenue that
leads

leads to the Caftle, and is, I believe, very well inclined to receive you favourably.

EARL OF LEWINGTON.

I'll attend him, and not lofe a fortunate moment.
[*Exit Lord Lewington.*

SIR WILLIAM.

Does my Jenny's gentle heart remain unalter'd by
this change of fortune ? or is it inclin'd to indulge
ambition at the expence of conftancy ?

JENNY.

Can fhe who lov'd thee as an obfcure villager,
reject thee as her brother's friend ?—Oh banifh the
fufpicion, Willy ; it is an unkind one.

AIR THE THIRTY-THIRD.

> Let fordid int'reft lead the bride
> Who weds thro' avarice or pride ;
> My foul thofe fofter paffions fway
> Which fhun Ambition's thorny way,
> And fondly chufe fome calm retreat,
> Where love and gentle friendfhip meet.
> [*Exeunt.*

Enter

Enter the EARL OF LEWINGTON *and* DON PEDRO.

[*They seem converfing as they enter.*

EARL OF LEWINGTON.

I prefume, Sir, you are acquainted with their writing; if you are, that Deed, which is fign'd by them both, will convince you of what I have related.

[*Giving a paper, which Don Pedro feems to read, while Lord Lewington goes to the fide-fcene, and returns leading Clementina.*]

DON PEDRO.

Infernal wretch !—Heavens ! and my fifter too !

EARL OF LEWINGTON.

[*Prefenting Clementina to Don Pedro.*
Your daughter, Sir !

[*Clementina kneels to Don Pedro.*

DON PEDRO.

[*Raifing and embracing her.*
Oh my child ! can you excufe an infatuated father, who wou'd have facrificed thy liberty and happinefs to a miftaken zeal ?

CLEMENTINA.

Can you, my ever honour'd father, pardon my difobedience in oppofing your commands ?

DON

DON PEDRO.

Yes, Clementina; and, as the only amends I can make for all the diſtreſs my ſeverity has occaſioned you, I give your hand where you've beſtow'd your heart. [*Preſenting her hand to Lord Lewington.*] With her, my Lord, accept a father's bleſſing; and may every felicity await you that love and fortune can beſtow!—With regard to the wretches who have ſo long impoſed on my too eaſy credulity, your Lordſhip is at liberty to act as you think proper—I renounce all friendſhip and alliance with them.

EARL OF LEWINGTON.

The favour I now receive from your hand, Sir, obliterates every former injury. And as to the Friar and Grizilda, the idea of their ſchemes being de-tected will be a ſufficient puniſhment; for an hypo-critical villain and an affected prude wou'd almoſt as ſoon forfeit their lives as their reputation.—I think I ſee them both coming this way, and, if you pleaſe, we will not take any notice of what has hap-pen'd, until we have diverted ourſelves a little at their expence. It will be as good as a farce to con-clude the evening.

DON PEDRO.

With all my heart: I ſhall enjoy their embar-raſſment exceedingly.

                                                Enter

Enter FATHER DOMINICK *and* GRIZILDA.

GRIZILDA.

Oh brother! I am glad you have found her.—By our Lady, I was afraid she had given us the slip.— [*She goes up to Clementina, and lays hold of her.*] Come, Mistress, you are once more safe in my hands, and I'll warrant, you never play me such a trick again.

DON PEDRO.

I don't believe she will, sister. But won't she think you cruel for endeavouring to confine her?— How wou'd you like such severity yourself, if you was in her situation?

GRIZILDA.

I in her situation, brother!—Did I ever disgrace my family by intriguing?—did I ever run off with a fellow in my life? — No; I defy the whole world to say one syllable against my character!

DON PEDRO.

Not so violent, sister—it will only increase your mortification presently:—but you are not the first of your sex that hid an amorous disposition under the mask of prudery.

GRIZILDA.

Brother, I won't be abused at this rate! that I
M   won't.

won't.—Father Dominick, will you ftand by and
hear me infulted, without taking my part? [*Afide to
Dominick.*] I'll be reveng'd on you if you do.

FATHER DOMINICK.

Sir, I am obliged to interfere, when an innocent
woman is injur'd in her reputation.—Your behaviour to that lady is unpardonable; and I muft tell
you——

DON PEDRO.

[*Interrupting Dominick.*

Hold, Dominick!—I'll be duped no longer by
your artifice. A full difcovery of certain villainous
intentions has open'd my eyes to conviction.—Have
you any remembrance of this paper, Dominick?
[*Shewing him the Deed Grizilda had dropp'd.*

FATHER DOMINICK.

S— S— Sir, I have left my f— f— fpectacles behind me, and I— I— I can't fee without them.—
[*Afide to Grizilda.*] Oh Lord! what will become of
us! It is our Agreement!

DON PEDRO.

Hold it a little nearer your eyes, and you may
perhaps know the hand at leaft.

FATHER DOMINICK.

Indeed S— S— Sir, it wa— wa— was not——

DON

DON PEDRO.

Your guilt confounds you, Dominick! but don't endeavour to extenuate one crime by the commiſſion of another.—Come hither, ſiſter : — Have you left your ſpectacles behind you too ?

GRIZILDA.

Oh dear, brother! don't expoſe me, and I will confeſs the whole plot.

DON PEDRO.

There remains nothing for you to confeſs. This paper reveals every circumſtance.

GRIZILDA.

Nay but, dear brother! do not make me appear ridiculous to the whole world :—conſider I am but a weak woman ; and it is no wonder I was prevail'd on by Father Dominick, when he told me it was all for the good of you and my niece.

DON PEDRO.

That artifice will not avail, Grizilda ; for falſe-hood only blackens the offence it is intended to palliate.—[*Turning to Dominick.*] As for you, Sir, for the ſake of many worthy men who wear that ſacred habit, I ſhall take care to ſee you ſtript of it. —Your villainies diſgrace your function.

M 2 FATHER

FATHER DOMINICK.

I was afraid it wou'd come to this as foon as I
heard of Queen Mary's death. However, the worft
that can happen is, that I muft e'en give up my new-
affumed occupation;—for, to fpeak the truth for
once in my life, all the divinity I have about me, is
contain'd in this outward garb of fanctification!

       [*Exit Father Dominick.*

GRIZILDA.

[*Afide.*] 'Tis well I have another lover in referye;
for poor Dominick is come off but fhabbily.

Enter SIR WILLIAM *and* JENNY,

[*Lord Lewington and Clementina meet them at the
further end of the ftage, and feem to converfe with
Jenny, while Sir William goes up to Grizilda,
and fpeaks in a clownifh dialect.*]

SIR WILLIAM.

Pray, ben't your name Dame Grizil?

GRIZILDA.

What! am I abus'd by you too?

SIR WILLIAM.

I thought you knew the dear obliging creature
never intended to deceive you!

       GRIZILDA.

GRIZILDA.

[*Slapping his face.*

Take that for your infolence, do!

CLEMENTINA.

Another lover, aunt? — Sure you never difgrac'd your family by intriguing!

GRIZILDA.

If I ftay among you any longer, I fhall burft with vexation and fury!—Wou'd I had you both in my power, you infolent minxes you!

[*Clementina and Jenny follow her finging, as fhe hobbles with her ftick to the further end of the ftage.*]

AIR THE THIRTY-FOURTH.

If a lover you wou'd obtain,
Calm your rage, your fury reftrain;
When a fair one's paffions rife
Like the ftormy ocean,
Anger flafhing from her eyes
Blafts the infant-paffion.

[*Exit Grizilda.*

DON PEDRO.

Now, my dear Clementina, if you pleafe, we will repair to the Caftle (as the approaching night makes this

this open situation rather unpleasant) and, though it is not so well provided for the reception of you and your amiable friends as I could wish, yet I hope a sincere welcome, and a good-humour'd host, will make some amends for indifferent entertainment.

EARL OF LEWINGTON.

The eye of felicity beholds every object in an agreeable point of view; and where happiness presides, as it does in our little circle, it diffuses an universal chearfulness around, and adorns the most homely scene with a thousand variegated beauties.

CHORUS the THIRTY-FIFTH.

May pleasures unbounded our union attend !
By Friendship enliven'd our transports extend !
Nor painful Suspicion, nor Jealousy wound,
But Hymen auspicious strew roses around !
While, blest by kind Fortune and favour'd by
    Love,
Mirth, wit, and good-humour our moments
    improve !   *[Exeunt omnes.*

END OF THE OPERA.

OLD

[175]

OLD TUNES,

To which the AIRS are adapted.

ACT THE FIRST.

Air
1. TWeedfide.
2. The Bullfinch,
3. When firft I faw thee graceful move.
4. ——— —— ———
5. Old Sir Symon the King.
6. The Serenade.
7. Handafyd's March.
8. The Padlock,
9. Pufh about the brifk bowl.
10. Ally Croker.
11. Fair Hebe.
12. The fool that is wealthy is fure of a bride.
13. Shawnbree.

ACT THE SECOND.

14. Rural Felicity.
15. Once more I'll tune my vocal fhell.
16. ═══════

Air

16. ————— ————

17. The heavy hours.

18. ———— ————

19. —————————

20. The laſt time I came o'er the moor.

21. ——————————

22. Daniel Cooper.

23. Batchelor Bluff.

24. Alas! too ſoon, dear creature.

25. Beſſy Bell and Mary Gray.

26. Drink to me only with thine eyes.

27. The Laſs of Patie's Mill.

A C T ᴛʜᴇ T H I R D.

28. Farewell to Lochaber.

29. Green grows the ruſhes.

30. Jolly mortals, fill your glaſſes.

31. ————— ————

32. Lady Coventry's Minuet.

33. No more ſhall meads be deck'd with flowers.

34. Rogue's March.

35. The laſt part of " If love's a ſweet paſſion."

F I N I S.